KT-489-686

Cheltenham

H-UA

Uniform with this volume

NOTTINGHAM *Geoffrey Trease*

SOUTHAMPTON *A. Temple Patterson*

READING *Alan Wykes*

GUILDFORD *E. R. Chamberlin*

In preparation

TYNESIDE *David Bean*

LEICESTER *Jack Simmons*

Cheltenham

A BIOGRAPHY

Simona Pakenham

Macmillan

© Simona Pakenham 1971

All rights reserved. No part of this publication may be reproduced or transmitted, in any form or by any means, without permission.

SBN boards: 333 10048 4

First published 1971 by
MACMILLAN LONDON LTD
London and Basingstoke
Associated companies in New York Toronto
Dublin Melbourne Johannesburg & Madras

Printed in Great Britain by
WESTERN PRINTING SERVICES LTD
Bristol

For
Celia and David

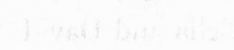

Contents

List of Illustrations

Grateful acknowledgements are due as follows:

To Cheltenham Art Gallery's museum for the use of photographs by the late Hugo van Wadenoyen (Plates 1, 15, 18–24, 30); and prints from their collection (Plates 7, 8, 10, 11, 12, 17, 26, 27); to Mr Eric Stokes for the loan of prints from his collection (Plates 3, 9, 14); to Mr R. A. Chiverton (Plates 2 and 32); to Miss Hampshire and the Governors of Cheltenham Ladies' College (Plate 28); to W. A. Bawden: Eagle Photos (Plate 16); to the Cheltenham Newspaper Company (Plates 13 and 25); to the Entertainments Manager and Cheltenham Borough Council (Plate 25); to Mrs Imogen Holst (Plate 31); and to the Eagle Star Insurance Company (Plate 33). Plates 4, 5, 6 are reproduced from Griffith's *New Historical Description of Cheltenham*, 1826.

LIST OF MAPS

ACKNOWLEDGEMENTS

To thank everyone who gave me help in planning this book would add another chapter and I do not even know the names of many who contributed ideas and facts – friends briefly made on the bus, in the parks or at shop counters.

My first and greatest debt is to Mrs Gwen Hart, who not only raised no objection to another author covering the ground of her massive *History of Cheltenham*, but advised me to save myself time by making use of her bibliography, which pointed out sources it would have taken me weeks to find on my own. I thank her, too, for permission to quote. I hope that this biography may interest people enough to send them to her much more detailed study of Cheltenham's early years – a book which is also a fascinating essay in the intricacies of local government.

Remaining in Cheltenham, my thanks are due to Mr Richard Board, M.B.E., one-time Deputy Town Clerk, for advice and help on the part of the town's history that comes within living memory. His reminiscences, in conversation and in letters, contained many vivid phrases he will recognize scattered about my text. Mr P. G. Mills of the *Gloucestershire Echo* also spared me much time and took great trouble to search out copies of articles which further shortened my work.

I had willing help from Cheltenham officials, and my thanks are especially due to Mr A. A. Crabtree, the Town Clerk, particularly for his exposition of the Town Plan. Mr W. Rust and Mr W. Gough, of the Municipal Offices, searched out maps and explained the intricacies of the Council estates. At the Library, Mrs Nancy Pringle was a mine of information, knowing exactly where to lay her hand on the relevant book or pamphlet. I am grateful for permission to reproduce part of her map of Cheltenham in 1617. In the Art Gallery, Mr G. H. Fletcher and his assistant, Miss D. A. L. Page, kindly let me rummage through their collection of prints and pictures at a moment most inconvenient for them, when they had them all stacked about the floor in preparation for the opening of the new Cheltenham Room.

In other areas of the town many people gave me valuable time, introductions and advice: Canon Hugh Evan Hopkins, O.B.E., M.A., Rector of Cheltenham; Mr G. A. M. Wilkinson, M.B.E., lately Entertainments Manager at the Town Hall, and Mr John Bullock, his successor; Mr Eric Stokes, with his marvellous collection of local prints; Mr A. D. Cozens of the Cheltenham Society; Miss M. S. Hampshire, Principal of the Ladies' College; Mr John Bayley, Agent for Corpus Christi; Miss E. F. Murray, Bursar of Pate's Grammar School Foundation; Mr Rae Hammond, Manager of the Everyman Theatre; Mr David Bannister; Mr Clifford Lee Lane; Mr Ronald Elgood; Mr H. G. Brittain, Manager of the Rotunda Branch of Lloyd's Bank; Mr and Mrs Reginald Pratley; Miss Sarah Beckley; Mrs Derrick of Chosen View and the teazel farming. I remember with particular pleasure many afternoons spent in reminiscence on every possible subject with Mr George Hannam-Clark.

Away from the town of the title, there are others to thank: Mr C. Day Lewis, once a Cheltenham College master and now adviser to the Literary Festival; Mr Ivan Mason, once a boy at Cheltenham College, and Mrs Helena Geldart, once a girl at the Ladies' equivalent; Mr Grahame W. Parker, Secretary of the Gloucestershire County Cricket Club.

I owe a very particular debt to Elizabeth Longford, who kindly sent me proofs of the Cheltenham episode of her *Wellington: the Years of the Sword* at a time when she was busy reading them herself, and for allowing me to quote; another to Miss Imogen Holst, for permission to quote from her biography of her father and for advice and information on her family's connection with the town.

Yet again I thank my husband, Noel Iliff, for exhaustive and exhausting (to both of us) readings of all stages of the typescript and for his many criticisms and suggestions, initially received with very bad grace, but later (generally) acted upon.

Lastly to my family in Cheltenham who put up with my frequent comings and goings. To my daughter-in-law, Celia, for soothing hospitality and good cooking; to my son, David, for stimulating hospitality and explanations of the mysteries of horse-racing; to my grand-daughter, Stephanie, for making my research easier by a succession of peaceful nights, rarely interrupted by the sort of disturbance expected from one of her age.

CHAPTER ONE

Personal Introduction

THE notices on the approach roads read 'Welcome to Cheltenham Spa' and your railway ticket will have the second word of the name printed on it, but during nearly all the time that I was writing there was not a drop of medicinal water to be had. While central heating was being installed in the restored and redecorated Pittville Pump Room there was a terrific thunderstorm. As a result of this, diesel oil from a broken pipe leaked into the only spring still in use and for two years Cheltenham was without the commodity that made it famous.

Ask a dozen people from the north, south or east of England what the name Cheltenham means to them and nine will reply – retired colonels, bath chairs, genteel ladies taking tea in the Promenade. Of the other three, one will not know; one will mention the Ladies' College; a third may have heard of the Music Festival.

A town's image, once fixed in the public mind, is hard to erase, and by the time it has been superseded the place may have passed to a new one. Cheltenham has had at least four, of which the present one has yet to be recognized. Its fame began just before the Regency, but while the celebrities of the nation were flocking there to take the waters or watch others take them, and the terraces of pillared and porticoed houses were springing up over the green slopes under the Cotswolds, people were still complaining of it as an insalubrious market, inhabited by a race of lawbreakers – a hangover from its days of illegal tobacco-growing. It took some time, in the mid-nineteenth century, for a clergyman who became as powerful in Cheltenham as Beau Nash was in Bath to alter the image of Regency

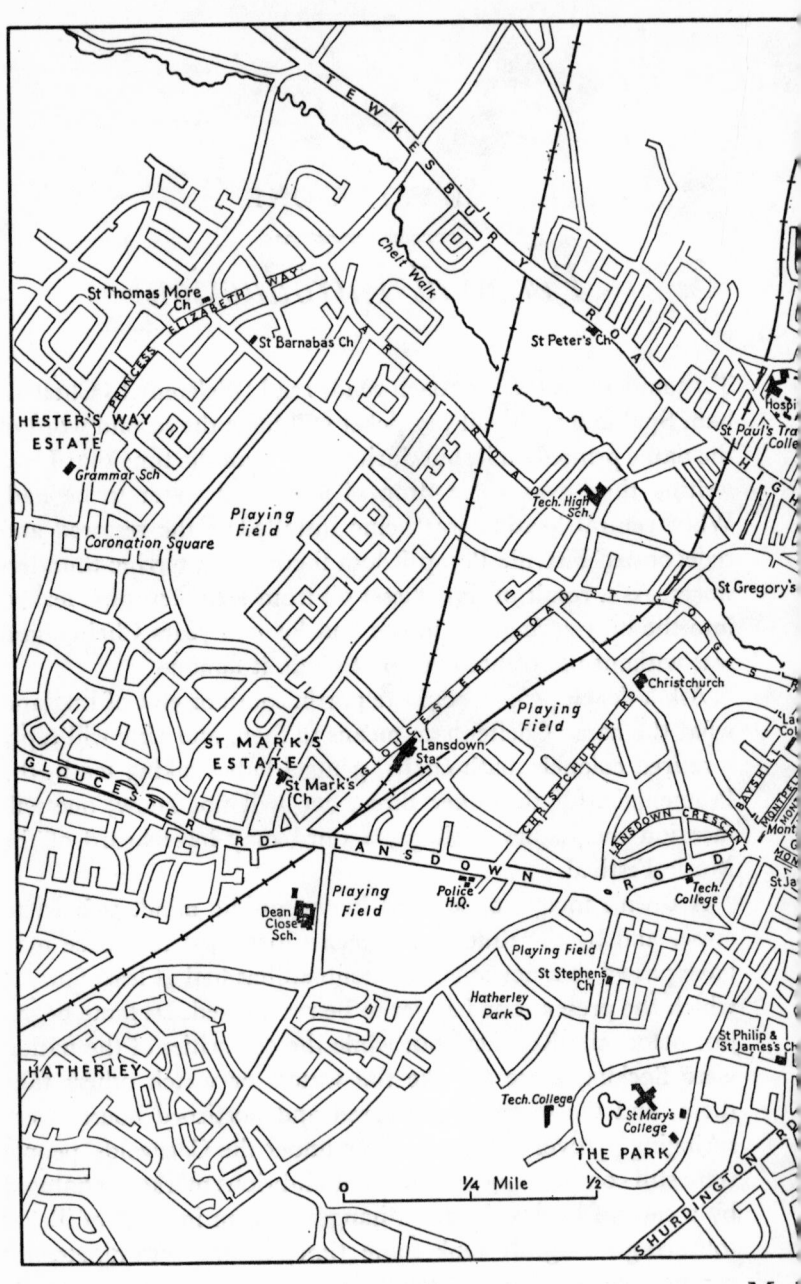

Mod

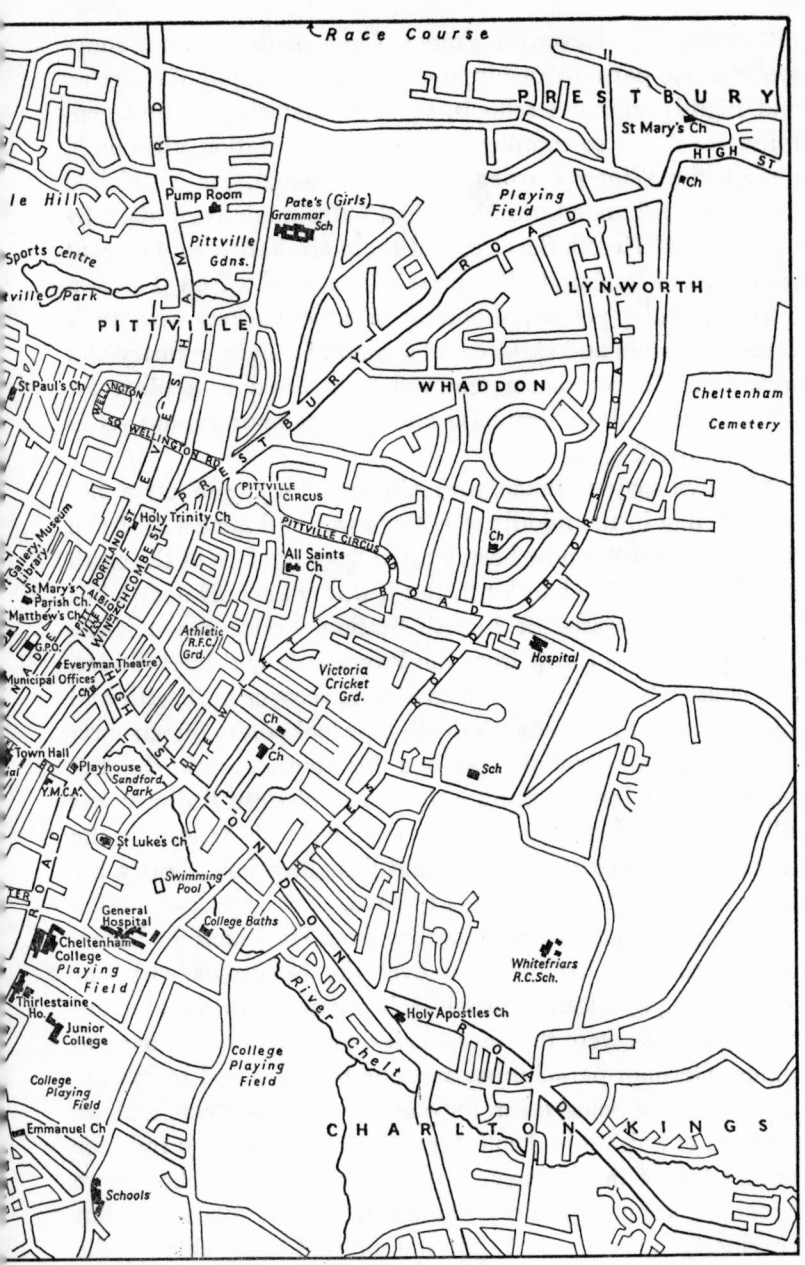

Cheltenham

rakishness. The Reverend Francis Close made it into Tennyson's 'polka, parson-worshipping place', a town full of churches
and slightly snobbish schools, strict Sabbatarianism and gen-
tility. He did it so thoroughly that this reputation still clings,
though the Winter Gardens are pulled down, the Municipal
Orchestra disbanded, the medicinal baths made redundant by
the National Health Service, and there are hardly any elegant
tea-rooms to be found. The present image, of a New Town, a
town of young people, shopping in supermarkets with their
hordes of babies and children, of a centre for light industry and
government departments removed from London, a place for
arts festivals with the emphasis on the contemporary, has yet to
establish itself.

My own acquaintance with Cheltenham began on a hot
summer day in the middle of Hitler's war and almost all I can
remember of it has now been blasted from the face of the earth
as if an atom bomb had hit it. But it was not enemy action but
Beeching that erased St James's Station – once conveniently
situated a stone's throw from the Promenade and High Street.
The house where Tennyson retreated to recover his health and
spirits after Arthur Hallam's death now looks on to fifteen acres
of grass-grown desolation. When his mother took the tall
mansion in St James's Square the Great Western Railway was
still building across the road and, as he wrote *In Memoriam*, the
future Poet Laureate can have had little idea how short a life
the new terminus was destined to have.

My husband and I were bicycling from Haslemere in Surrey
to Malvern and had climbed over the Cotswolds with our
holiday luggage, losing ourselves in attempts to avoid main
roads, for those were the days when signposts were removed to
confuse German parachutists and one hardly dared to ask the
way for fear of being taken for one. It was a long ride and we
proposed to finish it in comfort, putting our cycles on a train for
the last lap of the journey. Nothing could have looked more
welcoming than St James's Station in the late afternoon, but
the elderly booking clerk (all station staff were elderly, the
young ones having gone to the war) shook his head. Whatever
the timetables may have promised the last Malvern train had

gone at 3.30. We had to bicycle another twenty miles. It is perhaps not surprising that I remember nothing of that visit but the station in the evening light with Tennyson's house across the road and the Catholic church beside it.

In the next ten years I got to know the town better. It became my shopping-centre during holidays spent on the Cotswolds. Sometimes I freewheeled in past the thatched roofs of Prestbury village and pushed out again, laden with purchases, up the slow incline of Cleeve Hill on the Winchcombe Road. Sometimes I coasted luxuriously down Cleeve and made a detour round the pleasantly rural New Barn Lane to enter through Albert Road and Pittville Lawn with its hundred-year-old trees. The great houses were shabby with flaking paint from enforced wartime neglect, a sight that would have delighted Cobbett, who despised them and their rich owners. The aura of Victorian Sabbath still brooded over these; hardly a cat was to be seen on summer afternoons.

The town centre was always busy and, for a cyclist, as alarming to negotiate as any in Britain. I remember the High Street as already a hideous conglomeration; the pleasant contrast of the Promenade with its great planes and chestnuts and some hazard from the rookery over one's head; the astonishing metropolitan luxury of Cavendish House (the Harrods of the Middle West); antique bargains in Royal Well Place and at Mr Hoggett's in St George's Place; the pleasant airy tea-room on the upper floor of Boots; the spa water in plastic cups from the fountain in the Town Hall and an eccentric friend shocking the staff by taking out his glass to pour it into the radiator of his car.

On hot and lazy days I went out on the Evesham Road to avoid hills, past Regency houses hung with wrought-iron balconies and garlanded with their shadows on the stone or stucco, along streets plentifully bordered with trees and green grass-verges – the Garden Town of England advertised by the Victorian guide books when the waters had ceased to pull in the crowds of the Regency boom. Thank goodness the balconies and the fantastic iron porches had been spared, for I could see where delicate railings had been rooted up as a contribution to the War Effort – a misguided piece of patriotism.

On lazier, hotter days I might put the bike on a train, with more success than on my wartime visit, and chunter in a leisurely way round the skirts of the hills through Gotherington, Greet and Gretton to get out at Broadway and push the loaded machine up the shorter, steeper hill on to the Cotswolds. I thought of Cheltenham as particularly railway-minded, with this delightful line that took one to Stratford-upon-Avon, and the beautiful journey in the other direction, to Cirencester by way of Andoversford, Withington and Chedworth over uplands where the Romans built their villas. These were lines for the potterer, but Cheltenham was serious about trains with no less than three stations in its centre – five counting the ones in the suburbs. Between wars it had been served by the famous Cheltenham Flyer which for a brief time in 1932 was the fastest in the country, keeping up a speed of 87·5 miles per hour for seventy miles between London and Swindon. Such haste to arrive did not seem to square with the town's reputation for valetudinarian colonels.

Later I was to spend holidays in the town itself, having discovered the Music Festival, that surprising brain-child of George Wilkinson, the Entertainments Manager, who, while the war still continued, conceived stick-in-the-mud Cheltenham as the first of the Festival towns – four years before Edinburgh, six before Aldeburgh – and the only one almost wholly devoted to contemporary music. Originally for four days, in 1945, and quickly increasing to a fortnight, the Festival transformed the place each July, with famous conductors and soloists shopping in the Promenade, Vaughan Williams a yearly visitor at the Ellenborough Hotel and the Hallé Orchestra sunning itself in shirt-sleeves on the grass between the Town Hall and the Queens Hotel.

It was some years later that I got to know the other side of the place and saw it from a totally new point of view. With a son in a Government department, living in a new suburb, I came across a Cheltenham not yet known to the world outside – the Cheltenham of vast raw housing-estates, spreading out to nibble at the Green Belt on the plain towards Tewkesbury and Gloucester. Here was the Cheltenham of multitudinous factories, for new things like aircraft components, electric clocks, hydraulic equipment, plastics, nylon, and older products such as face lotion, church monuments, crumpets and beer – almost anything, indeed, that can be made in small, clean, not too obtrusive factories, without noise, smoke or public nuisance. This was the Cheltenham of the young and their fast-increasing families, newly built churches, schools and shops, blocks of flats (mercifully few and not too high) and semi-detached villas (innumerable) with new gardens all too often decorated with gnomes, and the usual forest of television aerials. Nearer the centre was the Cheltenham of multifarious activities and interests ('You name it, we have a society for it,' said the Information Office, despairing at being asked to reel off a list of several hundred to me); of Cricket Week and the Gold Cup (ancient) and the Literary Festival (comparatively new); the Cheltenham of the Samaritans, coping, from the parish church office, with a highish suicide-rate; of the couple of hundred hippies living, loving and smoking pot behind misleadingly cleaned up Georgian façades in Lansdown Crescent; of skin-head invasions at weekends.

Endlessly quartering the streets in fine weather and in wet, at every possible season, in search of facts and impressions, the town's biographer comes away with a curious selection. Cheltenham, it seems, has the world's dirtiest buses and the most uneven pavements. With eyes directed well above the ground to look at architecture she risks being precipitated flat on her face a score of times in an hour. Perhaps it does not seem worth while to flatten them while the town waits for the New Plan. If invalids and the elderly retired really did make up the bulk of the population the hospitals would be full of broken knees and noses. The buses are frequent, to the point that it hardly matters that they usually arrive late and start again before their scheduled time; but, late or early, all of them seem caked with dust, in which the enormous child-population has written caustic comments.

Out in the streets all day, the biographer feels the need, from time to time, of two amenities – quick, reasonable self-service cafés and adequate public conveniences. The former are remarkably hard to come by for a town of Cheltenham's size and non-existent on a Wednesday afternoon; the latter are reasonably numerous but not of the standard to be expected at a health resort. They exhibit a curious sidelight on the town's subconscious – where those for the two sexes stand side by side they are frequently labelled MEN and LADIES. Is it that gentlemen are in short supply, or could this be the subtle influence of the Ladies' College, whose tidy green-clad inmates are to be seen about the streets in early morning and late afternoon?

Of the things I had remembered most had changed, though the rooks still build without municipal interference in the trees of the Promenade and the air of Sabbath still hangs over certain areas – in the crescents of Lansdown hardly any life is to be seen between morning and evening except a quantity of learner drivers practising three-point turns in perfect safety. In spite of local panic about traffic problems the town centre seems, to a bicyclist, easier to negotiate than it was twenty years ago. This is partly because of new one-way-street patterns, partly because the Severn Bridge has diverted some of the heavy lorries that used to hurtle through. The High Street, with the new Sainsbury and Tesco where the Grammar School had stood since Tudor times, is more than ever hideous; the Promenade, by contrast, seems even more attractive; but Cavendish House, with a new façade, has succumbed to canned music; you would be a genius to discover an antique bargain even in the by-ways; Boots has suppressed its pleasant tea-room; the Ellenborough Hotel is no more, and, though a new well was being drilled all the time I was working on this book, there was no Spa water fit even for cars to drink.

One of the changes which shows the town is coming to accept its new identity is the capitulation in the 1960s of Cavendish House and other Promenade shops to Wednesday early closing. Having stood out, for years, for Saturday-afternoon closing, they are now trying to persuade the Borough Council to allow six-day trading. At present Saturday is the busiest day of all, with young families coming in from the housing-estates to shop in the Prom, and Cheltenham is as dead on Wednesday afternoons as a French town on a Monday.

But the most fundamental change is in the railways, that one-time Cheltenham glory. Drastically cut in the late 1960s, not without loud protest and the burning of Marples in effigy, only one of the five stations was allowed to remain, and that one inconveniently situated far from the centre. British Rail promised that Lansdown Road would be enlarged and beautified before St James and Malvern Road were swept away, but it is only in 1970 that a start has been made on renovating the dilapidated façade, long ago shorn of its handsome portico, and there is no sign of improvement to the platforms and waiting-rooms. As for the trains, they no longer break records, though Cheltenham is a dozen times busier with the nation's affairs than it was in the Flyer's day, and they appear to be designed for the rich or for the staff of Government Communications Headquarters, who have their fares paid for them, for first-class carriages outnumber second, which, on rush-hour trains, are insufficient for the number of customers. How Dean Close, that Victorian opponent of Cheltenham's railway projects, would triumph if he could visit the modern town!

The plight of the derelict St James's Station seems symbolical of Cheltenham's problems. For the writing of the town's biography one could not have picked a more interesting moment, or one more difficult than the present. There stands the open space, like those bombed sites that existed so long around St Paul's in the City of London, producing a wealth of wild flowers (and weed seeds) instead of the small fortune in rates that the Corporation should expect from fifteen acres near the centre. Like the owners of property, who cannot sell and do not know whether to repair or repaint, it waits for the new Town Plan. Cheltenham stands at a crossroads, in a state of suspension, having had its first Plan rejected (to the delight of all who care for the Regency town) and only now beginning on a second. The first wasted six years; the new one should take only fifteen months, but how many must pass before its recommendations, whatever they may be, can be implemented?

Everyone in Cheltenham, from the Town Clerk to the casual stranger on a park bench, seems eager to talk about the place. No one attempts to hide the fact that the Town Plans are the cause of passionate disagreement and ill-feeling. It will be impossible to write about Cheltenham's present and future without treading on somebody's toes. This is surely an excellent thing. To the uninvolved observer it appears that everyone is taking a healthy interest (even when it is self-interest) in what is going to happen and a picture emerges of a community very far removed from the elderly, genteel complacency that the outside world still conjures up when it hears the word 'Cheltenham'. Did such a community ever exist? History suggests that if it did it lasted little more than a decade or two and only in the richer parts of the town.

Before Victorian respectability imposed its image, before the days of Regency bucks, even before the rebellious tobacco growers of the seventeenth century, Cheltenham had had a long history, and of this only one relic remains – the splendid-spired parish church of St Mary, now hemmed in, in its pleasant oasis of grass and lime trees, behind the backs of shops and offices, approachable only on foot by six little pathways. This, with the line of the High Street and the River Chelt, which runs, some-times under, sometimes over ground, through stretches of park, behind gardens and orchards, through gasworks, back yards and bits of neglect and demolition, right across the town from east to west, is the place to search for the history of Cheltenham up till the time when the Regency builders moved in.

CHAPTER TWO

The Town under the Hill

CHELTENHAM made its first appearance in history as the bone of contention between two bishops. Spelt variously Cintenham and Celtanhomme it figured in a document at the Synod of Cloveshoe in 803, 'the seventh year of the reign of Genwulf, the pious king of the Mercians'. 'A contention (among much else) arose between Deneberht, bishop of the Church of Worcester, and Wulfhard, bishop of Hereford' on the subject of which had the right to the rents and profits of a monastery in that place. There must, therefore, have been a religious house where Cheltenham now stands since at least 773, for the Bishop of Worcester claimed to have been drawing its revenues for thirty years. The monastery is thought to have stood on the bank of the Chelt, in the part of the town known as Cambray.

The western descent of the Cotswolds that shelters Cheltenham was inhabited in prehistoric times and burial places have been uncovered – long barrows at the Crippets and Leckhampton Hill; earthworks on Cleeve Hill, with the remarkable Belas Knapp, a thousand feet above sea level, with the earliest example of local dry-stone walling, dated approximately 1400 B.C. The sites on the hills survive and can be visited, but most of the remains on the flat land have been ploughed up for farming or swallowed under the growing town. In 1832 a cromlech, three uprights and a massive capstone, was discovered by builders near the middle of the town. The capstone was taken to Knapp House where it was used as a cider press. In 1846 the Great Western Railway destroyed what remained of a round barrow while levelling ground to make an approach for traffic. Now, in its turn, the Great Western property has gone the way of the ancient burial place and been razed to the ground, and nobody knows, at the time of writing, what will be built on the waste ground that was once St James's Station.

No Cheltenham existed in Roman days, though the site became surrounded, in the years of occupation, by Roman habitations. The invaders came to Gloucester in A.D. 43 when the Emperor Claudius was in Britain. The place where Cheltenham was to be was sixteen miles north-west of Cirencester (Corinium), the second largest town in Roman Britain, built at the crossing of two great highways, Ermine Street, which joined London to Gloucester (Glevum) and the Fosse Way from Exeter to Lincoln. By the time the occupiers' power was declining a half-circle of villas existed on the Cotswolds above Cheltenham, from Winchcombe to Witcombe. A little beyond Withington are the remains of the best-preserved Roman villa in Britain, nestling in a coombe of the Coln valley at Chedworth. The complete layout has been uncovered, with its living-quarters, bath houses and beautiful tessellated pavements, and a separate temple for the nymphs who ensured its water supply.

After the civilizing Romans came the dark age of Anglo-Saxon conquest. Ceawlin, King of Wessex, defeated the Kings of Bath, Gloucester and Cirencester at the Battle of Deorham, and in 577 'Gloucestershire first felt the tread of Englishmen's feet'. The Saxons now commanded the Severn valley and could prevent the Britons of Cornwall joining the Britons of Wales in a counter-attack. A tribe of West Saxons made its home in the country that was to become Gloucestershire. Its people were known as the Hwiccii.

The next invader was Penda, the elderly, ambitious King of Mercia. He made the Hwiccii sign a treaty at Cirencester by which, in 628, Gloucestershire became part of his huge kingdom, which extended from the Wye to the Wash, the Humber to the Thames. Penda was pagan, but his sons became Christian converts. Christianity had all but died out at the time of the Saxon invasion, to be revived in 597 after Augustine's famous mission.

Two hundred years later Archbishop Theodore of Tarsus instituted the yearly Synod where the name Cintenham made its first appearance. By the ninth century many churches had been built in Mercia – the one at Worcester which was to become the cathedral; abbeys at Bath, Gloucester, Tewkesbury, Evesham, Pershore; monasteries at Winchcombe, Withington, Cleeve, Hatherley, Beckford, Deerhurst and Charlton. At an unknown date the one on the bank of the Chelt was erected, to be disputed over by the bishops of the new adjoining sees. It was during this period that the Venerable Bede was moved to complain that so much land was being given to the Church that hardly any was left for retired soldiers or the sons of noblemen.

A great silence now came down upon the future Cheltenham and nothing further is heard of the settlement under Cleeve Hill till after the Norman Conquest. The little priory was probably destroyed by the Danes, who swept away many churches near Gloucester before King Alfred defeated them at Ethandune in 877. Before the name was heard again the country had been divided into shires and hundreds, and Gloucestershire, annexed to the ruling house of England, had become part of Wessex. The Lord of the Manor was the King, the first recorded owner being Edward the Confessor.

The place did not appear in its modern spelling till it figured in the Manor Act of 1625 as 'Cheltenham Street'. It was variously written Chiltham, Chilteham, Chintenham, Chiltehe and Cheltham. The older guide-books attribute its name to the little stream which ran for several centuries through the middle of the High Street, but Gwen Hart, the town's twentieth-century historian, believes the river was named after the town, not the town after the river. *Chelt* being Anglo-Saxon for a cliff and *ham* for a settlement, Cheltenham was probably 'the town under the hill'. The Normans found vines in cultivation, for the site was sheltered. Gloucestershire monks became great growers of the grape. Alfred the Great described the place wistfully; how the surrounding forests provided the necessities for building – handles for tools and timber for houses 'wherein men may dwell permanently in peace and quiet, summer and winter, which is more than I have done yet'.

In becoming king, William the Conqueror became, automatically, Lord of Cheltenham Manor; and the Manor, being royal, gave its name to the hundred which contained it. With Westminster and Winchester, Gloucester was one of three centres of government in William's day, and it was only nine miles away, where he was sitting with the Witan in 1085, that he made the decision that led to Cheltenham's second mention in history. Wearing the crown and sitting with his archbishops and bishops, abbots and earls, thanes and knights at the midwinter session, he decided to survey the whole country, a move which led to the making of Domesday Book.

'*Terra Regis*. King Edward held Chinteneha,' read the completed survey of 1086, describing not only the Manor but the Hundred,

> There were eight hides and a half. One hide belonged to the Church: Reinbaldus holds it. There were three plough teams in demesne and twenty villani and ten bordarii and seven servi, with eighteen plough teams. The priests have two plough teams. There were two mills of 11*s* 8*d*. To this Manor King William's Steward added two bordarii and four villani and three mills. Of these two are the King's; the third is the Steward's, and there is one plough team more. In the time of King Edward it paid £9 5*s* and three thousand loaves for the dogs. Now it pays £20 and twenty cows and twenty hogs and 16*s* instead of the bread.

This description is not very helpful as nobody agrees on the extent of a 'hide'. A team of eight oxen could till about 120 acres. The mills along the river included Arle, Sandford and two at Alstone. The most famous of these, known later as Barrett's Mill, was at the pool still to be seen where the Chelt runs above ground through Sandford Park.

William's Steward had a bent for finance. Apart from adding three mills to the two of the Confessor's time, he increased the revenue by doubling taxes and yearly enriched the royal larder to the extent of forty carcases. William could have little opportunity to hunt the neighbourhood, so the payment of loaves for his hounds was profitably altered to a money tax. Only the male population was given in Domesday Book and amounted to 114. Gloucestershire villeins are reckoned to have held about 80 acres; bordars about 30.

'Reinbaldus', who held the church land, was a wealthy Norman who came to England before the Conquest with Edward the Confessor. After the religious fervour of the sixth and seventh centuries the Church had relapsed into lethargy and William's archbishop, Lanfranc, set about its reformation, putting Norman clergy in place of native ones. For a time Reinbald was Chancellor of England, a post in which he was able to accumulate a great deal of land, and, by his death, he held about seventeen livings. He was also dean of a college of canons in Cirencester and left most of his possessions to them. The Cheltenham living, however, reverted to the Crown. Its lands comprised Church Meadow, in which the Royal Crescent and the regrettable bus-station now stand, and Cambray Field, which, seven centuries later, was to become the most fashionable quarter of Regency Cheltenham.

Apart from replacing English priests with their own, the Normans set about rebuilding churches, large and small, in their solid, magnificent style. In an uneven circle round Cheltenham, moving north and then clockwise, the visitor can discover a quantity which are completely Norman or retain well-preserved Norman features – Swindon, Stoke Orchard, Bishop's Cleeve, Stanley Pontlarge, Postlip, Southam, Withington, Elkstone, Leckhampton and Churchdown.

Cheltenham's St Mary's 'with the lands thereof, and the mill, and the chapels and all other appurtenances', now belonging to the Crown, went back to join the rest of Reinbald's property when it was handed over by Henry I as part of an endowment to a new abbey being built at Cirencester by the Augustinians. This now held Reinbald's accumulated riches and his tomb with the inscription

> Hic jacet Reinbaldus Presbyter
> quondam hujus Ecclesias decanus et tempore
> Edwardi Regis Angliae cancellarius

Henry II was present at the abbey's dedication in 1176, when Cheltenham was one of seventeen churches supplied with priests from the college there. Their tithes went to the abbey and Cheltenham ceased to be accountable to the Bishop of

Worcester. It remained in this situation until the Dissolution of the Monasteries in 1539.

The Augustinians were passionate builders. They began the present church of St Mary in the mid-twelfth century. It was conventionally cruciform in shape, its nave the same length and breadth as it remains today, though the side aisles were no more than narrow corridors with low ceilings. The short central tower was supported on the same piers, shafts and capitals that today hold up its graceful spire. These pillars and the west wall of the nave are all that remain of the work of those first builders. A modern door in the west wall cuts through the original string-course, but the flat buttresses to either side of it are Norman. It was a large church for the size of the population, though it does not compare with the great churches of the Cotswold wool merchants, but it was designed to accommodate communicants from the chapels of Leckhampton and Charlton and the little chantries of Arle, Hatherley and Southam, to all of which it stood as Mother Church, and who, on certain days, had to gather at St Mary's.

As a royal possession the Manor enjoyed a number of rights, privileges and exemptions from the laws governing the rest of the country. The kings who were the successive lords sublet to various tenants. Henry III leased it for four years to its own inhabitants at £64 a year. 'Know ye', ran his writ to the Sheriff in 1226, 'that we have granted our men of Cheltenham our Manor of Cheltenham . . . and that neither ye nor your bailiffs are to have right of entry there . . . neither are ye to levy any fees or other money.' The lessees were given the right to hold 'one market each week on Thursday', a right which was to mark the beginning of Cheltenham's growth into a town. He gave permission for a three-day fair on either side of St James's day, an event which continued late into the nineteenth century. Thursday is still market day in Cheltenham.

In this way the town became a law unto itself, accountable to nobody but its Lord. The lords of the subsidiary manors in the Hundred seem to have adopted similar licence, for the Bishop of Hereford, who owned Prestbury Manor, was discovered, at a round-up of criminals in Henry III's time, to have set up a gallows for his private use. Its exact location is unknown, but the lane from Cheltenham to Prestbury was called Gallows Lane till the last century.

The 'Liberty of Cheltenham', as it came to be known, because of this singular exemption from laws affecting the rest of the kingdom, was almost unique, only the 'Liberty of Slaughter' on the Cotswolds having a similar charter. John Prinn, collecting records in the time of Charles II, described it: 'Within this manor are sundry ffranchises and libertys, which are very rarely found in any other manors within the realme; viz – to make justices of assize, justices of coram and peace, *custos rotulorum*, sheriffs, high and low – stewards, high and low – bailiffs of the borough – '. No authority outside the Hundred might presume to question these officers. The Manor Steward held yearly court for the trial and execution of criminals and their property was sequestered for the Lord. These rights, together with exemption from taxes, had been granted under charter in the time of Edward the Confessor.

All this, the Manor and its attendant privileges, Henry III handed over in 1247 to the Abbey of Fécamp and the Liberty of Cheltenham, with Slaughter, passed wholly out of English jurisdiction into that of an order of monks from Normandy. Fécamp, which already had monasteries in Gloucestershire, also owned 'alien houses' at Rye and Winchelsea. While England was still ruled by Norman kings the situation presented no difficulty, but after John lost Normandy it became increasingly hazardous for two of the Channel ports to be in the hands of a potential enemy. Henry therefore exchanged Rye and Winchelsea for Cheltenham and Slaughter. The Liberties were now freed even from the jurisdiction of the Crown and anyone who interfered in their affairs stood in peril of a fine of £100 to the Treasury. The situation had its complications. There was a dispute, for instance, over fruit trees planted by the Bishop of Hereford, and the Abbot of Fécamp had to be instructed either to have the fruit gathered on the Bishop's behalf or to allow him to send his bailiff in to pluck it. Cheltenham's curious position did not remain unchallenged. There were frequent objections that the conditions in the Liberties 'hinder justice and

undermine royal authority, because they obey neither the
itinerant justices nor the king's servants'. But the abbots were
able to prove their case against all complainants and in 1367
Edward III was compelled to define their rights more precisely.

There is no suggestion that the abbots bothered to cross the
sea to inspect their property, but they did not neglect to send
monks to gather the useful revenues. The Liberties were briefly
confiscated during periods of war with France until Henry IV
burnt Fécamp. It was Henry V who eventually put an end to
the complicated situation. Before invading France in 1415 he
confiscated all foreign-held property and gave Cheltenham
Manor to his aunt, Elisabeth of Huntingdon, for her lifetime. On
her death it went as part of his endowment to the convent of Syon
– a religious house he founded at Twickenham as an act of repentance for his father's complicity in the murder of Richard II.

While the Liberty of Cheltenham existed as an island in the
middle of England ruled by a French abbot, the church, with
its 240 acres, continued to belong to the Abbot of Cirencester
and constituted, therefore, 'a Liberty within a Liberty'. A
situation of unparalleled oddity existed, with the people paying
taxes to a foreign cleric, going to church at the instruction of an
English one, and paying no service, either in money or obedi-
ence, to the Bishop of Worcester in whose diocese they lived.
The building of the church continued slowly and was not completed until the fourteenth century, by which time there had
been many alterations in the style of ecclesiastical architecture.
Unlike that of its great neighbour, Tewkesbury Abbey, the
intended square tower was not finished by the time the Norman
style was superseded. The discovery of 'ribbed vaulting' made it
possible to increase height without having to lengthen existing
supports, and new-style pointed arches were built, springing up
from the original short pillars of the crossing. The chancel was
not begun till late in the building programme, by which time it
was the fashion to make chancels larger, a fact which accounts
for its disproportion to the nave. It is also out of alignment with
the nave and is believed to have been built over the foundations
of the original Saxon church. If this is so, the piece of ground it
covers has been consecrated for worship for about 1200 years.

At the beginning of the fourteenth century the nave and its narrow aisles were pulled down, leaving only the west wall, and rebuilt inside the proportions dictated by this and the pillars of the crossing. The aisles were widened, almost obliterating the original cruciform plan, for the transepts hardly now project beyond the walls of the nave. An octagonal broach spire, 167 feet high, was set on the foundation of the abortive tower. The new building was of the Decorated character, with ball-and-flower ornaments, the corbels supporting the ceiling being carved with grapes and vine leaves which recall the vineyards planted by the early monks in the shelter of Cleeve Hill. The large windows must have let in plenty of light and are adorned with tracery exhibiting nearly every variation of medieval invention. Their rich patterns can best be seen now from outside. Inside their lines have been obscured and the church made poky and dark by the sentimental enthusiasm of wealthy Victorians who conspired to fill them with highly coloured memorial glass.

The new owner of the Manor under Henry V was the head of a Brigettine order, an abbess who ruled over seventy-seven nuns, priests and deacons in the new convent at Twickenham. She held all the powers granted by the Confessor's charter and, in addition, while Henry lived, was exempt from paying tax to the Crown. Like Fécamp's abbots, she did not visit Cheltenham, nor is it likely that her nuns travelled there, for the Brigettines were an enclosed order, vowed to silence; but the convent kept a staff of laymen to look after its business. Successive abbesses ruled Cheltenham for a hundred years, during which time Syon became one of the richest abbeys in the land. Its wealth was its downfall, causing it to be one of the first religious houses suppressed by Henry VIII. Inquiring into monastic finance, he found its yearly income was £1731 8s 4½d, of which £79 1s 8d came from Cheltenham. By the time the affairs of Syon had been wound up the Abbey of Cirencester had also been razed to the ground. The Dissolution of the Monasteries brought sweeping changes, therefore, not only to the Manor, which reverted to the Crown, but also to the parish church of Cheltenham.

CHAPTER THREE

Absentee Landlords and Troublesome Tenants

IN the hundred odd years between the time when Henry V handed the Manor to the Abbess of Syon and Henry VIII took it back again, Cheltenham only made one appearance in history. In 1471 the Lancastrian army, led by Margaret, wife of the imprisoned Henry VI, came from Bath 'in a foul country, all in lanes and stony ways, betwixt woods, without any good refreshing'. Holinshed records that Edward IV, on his way to meet the Queen 'came to a village called Cheltenham, where he had certain knowledge that his enemies were already come to Tewkesbury, and were incamped there, preparing to abide in that place and to deliver him battel'. The King did not stay to rest, but marched his 3000 Yorkist men straight to the Bloody Meadow, and there, on 3 May, the Wars of the Roses ended. Margaret was defeated and her young son, Edward, the Lancastrian heir, murdered on the field, some said by his uncles, the Dukes of Clarence and Gloucester.

Cheltenham had been listed as a borough in 1336, while still in the government of Fécamp. Henry III's charter had led to its expansion into the 'long towne havynge a market' later described in Leland's survey for Henry VIII. What became the High Street ran from above the church towards the mill in present-day Sandford Park. The stream ran south of the town. The Manor House, where Syon's Steward and Bailiff held court, was situated near the present Police Station and St Matthew's Church. Accounts for repairing it still exist – charges for mending the roof and walls and for cement for the rotting foundations. A new Hall and Crosse Chamber was built in 1459 and the cost of its erection was detailed to the last penny, 'nails, 12s. 5½., crestes [tiles?], 9s. 8d., straw, 1s. 6d'.

For a picture of Cheltenham life in the hundred years before the Reformation the collection of Court Rolls, accounts of sessions at the Manor House, is the only authority. The courts dealt with crime and matters which would now come under local government. The Steward was a man of substance and rank; the Bailiff looked after the agricultural work of the Manor and kept its accounts. It was a farming community. In Domesday time and after, all types of tenant – freemen, who lived on inherited land, copyholders, and tenants in demesne – were expected to work so many days in the year on the Manor farm. Richard Greene, for example, held about 15 acres, paid a rent of 4s, and owed the following service; a day's hoeing, a day's mowing and a day for lifting the hay. He had to provide a man at his expense to make haycocks, and another to work with him three days in autumn. He paid the Abbess 2d when he sold a horse; 1d a year pannage for each of his pigs to feed in her woods and ½d each for piglets. He had to pay for licence to marry his children, and when he died his best animal was given as heriot before his sons could succeed to his holding. As the village grew into a market town certain craftsmen were released from field labour to follow trades useful to the community and gave money in lieu of time – Greene's assessment for his work being 2s 1d. Cheltenham's craftsmen included thatchers, slaters, carpenters, weavers, millers, bakers and brewers, so the settlement was virtually self-supporting. Timber came from Charlton Kings, which provided firewood for visitors, material for tumbrils and market stalls, and a ducking-stool for scolds or dishonest tradesmen.

All the men of the Hundred, including the absentee lords of the subsidiary manors, were bound to attend the half-yearly courts or pay a fine, varying from a goose to a couple of draught oxen according to their means and station. A court of Pie Powder was held at the market where offenders in commerce, buyers or sellers, could be dealt with on the spot. The crimes tried before the Manor included common matters like burglary, assault and battery, but offenders were arraigned, besides, for fouling the water supply, for selling short-weight bread or substandard ale. Cheltenham has been a centre for brewing from early times and a licence of a penny in the Borough and of threepence in other parts of the Hundred was exacted from anyone desiring to make beer. The product had to be submitted to an official aletaster and fines for brewing without licence or for inferior ale brought so much profit that little attempt was made to encourage men to keep the rules.

Fields were enclosed from spring to autumn for the growing of crops, but after harvest were thrown open as common land where all tenants could pasture their beasts. In the period of enclosure it was an offence to allow cattle to stray, and the erring animals were impounded near the Fleece Inn to be released on payment of a fine. There were fines for poaching in the Lady's woods and warrens or fishing in her ponds. The medieval system of law persisted in Cheltenham long beyond most English towns, and, as late as the 1920s, there was still a Steward of the Manor to whom the Lord's tenants continued to pay heriot.

The Church also collected dues and exacted penalties. On a tenant's death the Abbess of Syon took possession of his best beast and the priest collected the second best on behalf of the Abbot of Cirencester. Tithes were due to the Church and were paid under protest. Adultery, slander or the failure to pay tithes were the principal sins dealt with by the consistory courts. In these matters the town differed little from others of its size. It was the possession of its own coroner and gallows and the exemption from duty to the Crown that set the Liberty apart.

In another circumstance Cheltenham was unlike other boroughs. The Manor House where the Steward held court was not the typical Great House with an aristocratic family to which people could look. Its Lord or Lady being absent, the town lacked a focus for loyalty. The great families lived at the subsidiary manors, chief among these being the Grevilles of Arle Court, descended from William Grevel, whose magnificent brass in the chancel floor of Chipping Campden church is inscribed with the legend 'the flower of the Wool Merchants of England'.

Although the Abbess of Syon was drawing nearly £80 a year from Cheltenham when Henry VIII intervened to possess himself of its wealth, the town was by no means prosperous. After Henry V's death it was no longer exempt from taxes, but in 1441 it was excused them along with Andover, Seaburgh and Headington, on account of poverty. War with France had put up taxes. The Wars of the Roses caused the price of land and the value of market tolls to fall. The Bailiff found difficulty in collecting rents due to the Manor. As often happens in time of poverty, some energetic farmers and craftsmen contrived to better their situation, buying land that fell vacant on the death or ruin of poorer tenants, and by the time of the Reformation a new class of prosperous burgesses began to appear.

Before the dissolution of Cirencester one last addition had been made to the parish church in the shape of a north porch. This had an upper chamber over it, reached by a narrow stair, a feature almost unique in church architecture, which probably served as a room where the priest could spend the night, keeping an eye on the sacred vessels. The parish priest was not the only official who conducted worship there. Two chantries had been established in the middle ages with legacies to support priests to say mass in perpetuity for their founders and all Christian souls – Our Lady's chantry and that of St Katherine. Both had their altars in the transepts, together with the necessaries of Catholic worship. The south transept still has the piscina and the aumbry which belonged to one of them. The rose window in the north transept was probably inserted to commemorate St Katherine's martyrdom on the wheel. The chantry priests were paid £4 to £5 a year and had 'no other lyving but the said service', but they are likely to have assisted the parish priest and taken their turn on watch in the north porch gallery.

The dissolution of Syon came about in 1539, with the confiscation of its revenues and the pensioning of the Abbess and her nuns at sums varying from £200 to £6 a year. The next year saw the destruction of Cirencester, one of forty-three monasteries in Gloucestershire. St Mary's, Cheltenham, with its land, the houses on it, the mill and the tithes went to Henry VIII. In 1541, a year of reorganization for the whole Church,

Cheltenham was removed from the diocese of Worcester and placed under the rule of the nearer see of Gloucester, where it remains to this day.

The effect of the Reformation was a drastic curtailment of religious ceremony. No candles were hallowed at Candlemas; no ashes on Ash Wednesday; creeping to the Cross was forbidden on Good Friday; no fire allowed at Easter but the one Paschal taper, no procession and no Cross. Mass books were burnt, images of the Virgin and the Rood removed, wall paintings whitewashed over, the piscina not used, the sanctus bell silenced. Bishop Hooper declared that 'an honest table decently covered' was preferable to an altar. To oblige him the shrines of the saints were removed and the ancient stone altar covered. The building was allowed to fall into a state of dilapidation.

There was a brief return to the abandoned ceremonies in Bloody Mary's reign, with services again in Latin. Hooper went to the stake in Gloucester, and Latimer, who had been Bishop of Worcester in the last few years that Cheltenham belonged to that see, was burnt at Oxford. Cheltenham's own martyr, recorded in Foxe's famous book, was John Cobberley, burnt at Salisbury for 'diverse heresies and false opinions'. His wife, Alice, recanted at the last moment, returned to their home town, married again and made successful claim for the return of her first husband's 'messuage and 14 acres of land'.

The history of Cheltenham's Grammar School had begun in the time of Mary's father. Shortly before his death in 1548 Henry VIII had a further fancy to augment his income and his acquisitive hand fell on the property of the endowed chantries of the realm; but the chantry priests, Edward Grove and Thomas Ball, were allowed to remain as curates. When Edward VI succeeded, commissioners were sent to assess chantry property in Gloucestershire and listed the 'houseling people' – communicants – of Cheltenham as 600. They charged Grove, by a covenant between the 'parysshoners of the said towne . . . always to teache their children, whiche towne is a markett towne, and much youthe within the same, nere unto whiche is no scholle kept. . . . It is thought convenyent to signyfye unto your worshippe the same be a meate place to establish some teacher and erect a Grammar Scole so it might stand within the Kynges Maiestie's pleasure.' The local record notes: 'Paid to Sir Edward Grove, schoolmaster, for his wages £5.' Sir Edward was not, of course, a member of an order of chivalry. Like Shakespeare's Sir Nathaniel he bore the courtesy title bestowed in Tudor times on clergymen.

One of the boys who went to Grove's little class was Richard, son of Walter Pate of Cheltenham. Little is known of his early life, but he steps into the limelight as a scholar of Corpus Christi, Oxford, going on to Lincoln's Inn where he was called to the Bar. He became Member of Parliament for Gloucester and the city's Recorder. He must have kept a pleasant memory of his Cheltenham schooldays, together, perhaps, with painful recollections of the school's inadequacy, for he formed an ambition to endow a permanent free grammar school in the place. Queen Elizabeth I placed the chantry revenues at his disposal and he made these over to Corpus Christi in 1574 on condition that three-quarters of the income should go to the upkeep of a school in Cheltenham and an almshouse for six poor old people, of whom two should be women. The new schoolhouse, which accommodated fifty boys, was a long stone building on the north side of the High Street where Sainsbury's and Tesco's new supermarkets now stand. Pate knew his Cheltenham and its people and made a wise decree that only four of the scholars should be taught both Latin and Greek; only five be expected to learn Latin to the extent that they could translate from English; while eighteen others might be given a minimum of instruction in that useful language. He understood the demands made on a boy by his parents, and decreed that the entrance fee of fourpence, the only payment required, must be paid again if the child went absent without leave for four days 'especially in time of harvest'. Boys from other parishes paid eightpence and the money was used to 'buy and provide such Latin and Greek books as shall be necessary . . . to be tied with little chains of iron'. The schoolmaster received £16 a year, the profits of the field adjoining the schoolhouse, and the right to feed his cow on the common pasture.

Cheltenham had its first resident Lord of the Manor in Elizabeth's reign – William Norwood of Leckhampton, the transcripts of whose lawsuits tell a great deal of the town's early history. The parish church continued, however, as a foundation separate from the Manor. Its Impropriations – that is, 'lands, houses, meadows, pasture, rents, etc. . . . . fines, heriots, mortuaries and reliefs, all tithes of fruit and grain, all profits and all royalties' – were let to various people who were obliged, in return, to support two 'fit and discreet chaplains and two deacons', to find bread and wine for the sacrament, provide straw and ropes for the bells, and see that the chancel was kept in repair. The church had returned to the reformed religion and Cranmer's Book of Common Prayer and the Act of Uniformity had been accepted in Gloucestershire without much opposition. Richard Pate was a Protestant, but Norwood, Lord of the Manor, whose portrait and whose lawsuits convey the impression of a contrary turn of mind, was listed as one of the only three Cheltenham people who failed the Act's obligation to attend regularly at church.

In 1597 Elizabeth leased the impropriation to her Lord Chancellor, Francis Bacon, Lord Verulam. Busy with official duties, the writing of his essays and (as some insist) Shakespeare's plays, Bacon was as much an absentee landlord as the former abbots and abbesses. He sublet to Mrs Elizabeth Baghott – a move that was to land him, the parish and the ecclesiastical authorities in a sea of trouble. Mrs Baghott was a character. Little is known of her beyond her clashes with the law, but she emerges as the first real personality in the little settlement descended from the Anglo-Saxon Hwiccii. She came of a family of cloth merchants, and her first husband was a Higgs from Charlton Kings. Prosperous and well connected, she had a nephew who became Attorney-General to James I's eldest son. Mrs Baghott's name appears in the Court Rolls with monotonous regularity, for neglecting hedges and ditches and for picking quarrels with her neighbours. John Stubbes, Norwood's under-steward, preserved a detailed record of her misdeeds and mismanagement of the church land.

Bacon first let the Rectory to Thomas Higgs, who quickly

was in trouble for allowing the chancel to decay and failing to distribute a fortieth part of the revenues to the poor. His widow, remarried, became a sworn enemy to Stubbes and was no more generous. There were nearly 2000 communicants by now and Mrs. Baghott was reaping £400 a year from her contract with Bacon, but she obstinately refused to pay the ministers more than £10, with a miserly 26s 8d for the deacons. The church, in consequence, could not recruit parsons of any learning and the preaching was deplorable. Stubbes approached Dr Parry, Bishop of Gloucester, to intervene. The Bishop came, preached in the church, and argued with the formidable lady, but even he could not persuade her 'by fair means or by threats, to increase the said stipends'.

The next move was an appeal from the Lord Treasurer. Signing himself 'Your loving friend', Lord Salisbury wrote to Mrs Baghott, more in sorrow than in anger, 'Whereas you are bound to maintain at your own costs and charges, two discreet chaplains and two deacons . . . you have, notwithstanding, maintained only two reading ministers there with the only allowance of £10 a year, to the scandall of the church and the defrauding of his Majesty's subjects of the spiritual food of their souls.' He promised not to call her to account if she reformed her behaviour or else made 'speedy repaire unto me to the court, to show what reason you have to continue in such an abuse'.

Luck was on Mrs Baghott's side, as happened all too often in her life. Evidently shaken by this missive, she instructed her nephew to make conciliatory overtures at Court, and promised to raise the stipends to £20, but Salisbury died before she had to implement this agreement and the Bishop of Gloucester was removed to another see. She was able conveniently to forget the matter for the time being.

The parish next appealed to Bacon against his penny-pinching lessee. He wrote at once to the lady.

Although you have given me cause to call you to account, for breach of your covenant . . . yet have I thought it good at this time to admonish you thereof, and to require you presently to reform the said abuses, by allowing two such discreet chaplains as shall be no'iated by His Majesty . . . £40

yearly unto either of them and duly to perform the covenant
of the said lease, so as there be no further cause of complaint
in that behalf against you. So, expecting your conformity
herein, without delay, I bid you farewell.

In echo of the Lord Treasurer, he signed himself, 'Your loving
friend'. Fortune was again on Mrs Baghott's side. Before she had
sent her answer, a matter in which she did not show great
haste, Bacon had been removed from office on charges of
bribery and corruption. Mrs Baghott did not long survive her
landlord, for the next recorded complaint in the parish was
directed against her sons, John and Thomas Higgs.

The £40 eventually received by Cheltenham's ministers had
to suffice their successors for many years to come, for a book
published in 1863 quotes Goldsmith on the incumbent being
'passing rich with forty pounds a year'. The period after the
Reformation was a sorry time for the Church. Before his
martyrdom Latimer had said in a sermon, 'We of the clergy
had too much, but that is taken away, and now we have too
little. . . . The poor clergy, being kept on a sorry pittance, are
forced to put themselves into gentlemen's houses, and there to
serve as clerks in the kitchen, surveyors, recorders, and other
offices of the like kind.'

CHAPTER FOUR

Civil War and Tobacco

THE penury of Cheltenham's Perpetual Curate (he was not a
Rector, though the church property is referred to as the
Rectory) was reflected in the condition of the Borough at the
end of Elizabeth's reign. It had been sending two Members to
Parliament, but the Queen excused the town the expense of
their journeys and subsistence on account of its poverty. There
had been bad times when she was on the throne; scares of a
Spanish attack on the Severn estuary had the train-bands
alerted and the beacon ready on Cleeve Hill; rumours that
Philip of Spain wanted to destroy the Forest of Dean because it
contributed timber for shipping. There had been a disastrous
year of plague in 1593, when the curate had entered four times
as many burials as baptisms in the parish register.

It was fully sixteen years after the dispute with Mrs Baghott
before the ministers of Cheltenham and Charlton actually saw
the £40 they had been granted. It was not till the Higgs' lease
had ended and Sir Baptist Hicks, who bought the impropriation
from James I, took over the right to appoint the clergy. Hicks
was a rich London merchant who had several times saved the
King in a financial crisis, in recognition of which the following
grant was made: 'our Rectory and Church in Cheltenham and
our Chapel at Charlton Kings . . . and our Church at Campden
. . . to Baptist Hicks who has well and truly paid large sums at
the receipt of our Exchecquer'. Sir Baptist was a man of taste
and imagination, but it is in Chipping Campden, where he
chose to build his mansion, that his principal mark is left. There,
about sixteen miles north-east along the edge of the Cotswolds,
his magnificent family chapel can be seen in the church, while

the rest of the town has memorials to him in the market hall and the strangely shaped gateway and fantastic pavilions that remain round the site of his vanished house. Hicks gave the right to nominate Cheltenham's ministers to Jesus College, Oxford, on condition that the stipends remained at £40 and the nominees should be unmarried Masters of Arts of two years' standing who held no other benefice. Jesus is a Welsh college and the consequence of Hicks's action can be seen in the list of incumbents. Up till the nineteenth century, when the right passed into other hands, it records a succession of Joneses, Howells, Lloyds, Llewellins and Hughes, with other names equally, though not so immediately recognizable as, Welsh.

Hicks's Cheltenham property comprised about 224 acres and 'the fair parsonage house', at the opposite end of the Street, 'acommodated with outhouses, a large barn, oxhouse, stables . . . a garden and a little orchard'. It also had 'a meadow with a fishpond in it adjoining the site of the Rectory called Cambray Meadow'. Near the church itself was a large pasture 'commonly called Church Mead'. At the beginning of the Stuart period a number of surveys combine to give a picture of Cheltenham's population and the life they lived before the Civil War. Besides John Stubbes's careful records there is 'Men and Armour', a list compiled by the Steward of Berkeley Castle, giving the name of every man capable of military service in the hundreds and hamlets of Gloucestershire, with details of his condition and capability – 'fitted to carry a musket, a caliver, a pike'; 'of mean stature, fit only for a pioneer'. He also recorded their professions, listing in Cheltenham about 128 people working on farms and fields and 28 as servants in the great houses. There were 6 tanners, 13 shoemakers, 13 tailors and 12 weavers; 12 maltsters, and 1 cooper to make casks for the local ale; 8 carpenters, 6 butchers and 4 bakers; one each of chandlers, smiths and wheelwrights, and 1 scrivener. In 1617 the lease to William Norwood expired and the Manor once more reverted to the Crown, when John Norden made a survey for the royal landlord. This spoke of two 'Market Houses within the Towne'. The principal of these stood on the north of the High Street opposite the Plough Inn. There was a High Cross in the street near the

entrance to the present Promenade and near it a small prison.
A Plough was already in existence, for the Gloucester consistory
court records a case of slander in which one woman accused
another of lying in wait for her husband outside its doors. North
of the Street, the part which now stretches out to Pittville, was
common land known as the Marsh, and it was here the schoolmaster was privileged to pasture his cow.

Apart from farming, the town's chief profit came from the
market, and the sale of shoes, leather goods and clothing can be
inferred from the high proportion of tanners, shoemakers and
tailors for the size of the population. The tenants of the houses
along the only street were responsible for its upkeep and cleaning. Each had to pave his frontage to a width of two yards and
clean this area on Wednesdays for the morrow's market. Three
times a week water from the Chelt was diverted to run down
the middle of the street to assist the cleaning. Each mill owner
was required to allow water from his pond to run out on certain
days and for this purpose had a sluice or wooden board with
three holes cut in it. There were continual lawsuits over the
millers' failure to comply with this obligation.

The law was frequently invoked over nuisance from dogs –
'for there cannot go into the street neither man, woman nor
child, nor beast nor pig without hurt or danger to life . . . but
shall be devoured with these mastiffs in the town of Cheltenham.' In the time of malt-making there was constant danger
from fire, and every person with a licence to brew was compelled
to provide 'one or more buckets of leather, to be ready in their
houses against casualty', while the rest of the town had to con-
tribute towards ladders and fire-fighting equipment. Barley and
oats were the principal crops and there were flocks of sheep,
though Cheltenham was not a wool town like the ones on the
Cotswolds above. Henrietta Street, north of the parish church,
was known as Fleece Lane until the nineteenth century.

By the time Norden began his survey another crop was
growing where the monks had once cultivated the grape, and a
guide book of 1863 speculated on how Cheltenham must have
appeared to a traveller of two centuries earlier; 'how strange a
sight must have been presented to his view – a few houses with

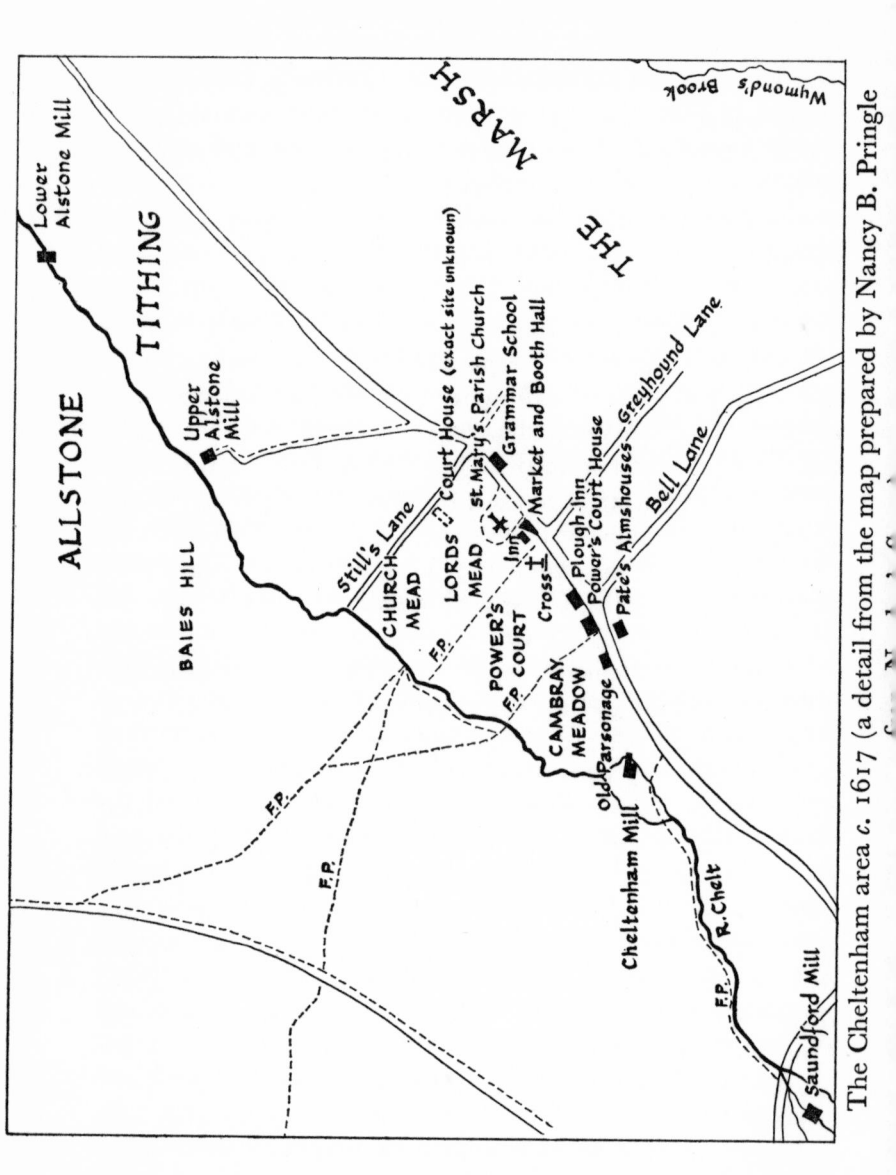

The Cheltenham area c. 1617 (a detail from the map prepared by Nancy B. Pringle

a running stream in their front forming the High Street and the land on either side planted with tobacco'.

The Fragrant Weed traditionally imported by Sir Walter Raleigh was first cultivated on the Cotswolds near Winchcombe. In James I's reign a grower gave evidence that 'he did betake himself into the country of Gloucester where poor folk do much abound, and there in one year planted so much tobacco as the poor had from the work of that year's crop £1500 or upwards'. The mild damp climate below the Cotswolds was even more favourable and it was not long before the broad leaves of *nicotiana* were waving in the summer meadows round Cheltenham, Gotherington and Tewkesbury.

James I, a king not noticeably fastidious in every matter, detested the smoking habit, which he attacked in his anonymously published *A Counterblaste to Tobacco* as a 'custom loathsome to the eye, harmful to the brain and dangerous to the lungs'. But the customs duty on the herb imported from the West Indies induced him to turn a blind eye to the beastly practice of pipe smoking so long as it was not in his presence, and he put a tax of 6s 8d a pound on the unpleasant stuff. He was later compelled to reduce this to a shilling because of the large-scale smuggling that resulted. The growing of tobacco in England, which had come as a godsend to the poor farmers of Cheltenham, was quickly found to interfere with vested interests. It reduced the revenue to the Crown, offended the Bristol importers and outraged the people of Virginia and Bermuda who had been given the sole right to send it to this country. In 1619 the King issued a proclamation making its cultivation illegal, but it was fifty years before the officers of the Crown were able to stamp out attempts by Gloucestershire growers to make a living from this profitable crop. Descendants of the obstinate Higgs and Baghotts of the country were not likely to give way without a struggle, especially as bad roads and difficult communications with the capital were on their side. Frequent messengers arrived bearing orders to destroy the crops, but the people of Winchcombe and the flat land below continued to cultivate their fields, passing off their produce on the London market as the genuine tobacco of Virginia and

Bermuda. The sheriffs and justices who received the orders to
wipe out the plantations were profitably growing it themselves,
and the coming of the Civil War, when the Government was
too busy to harry a small community of lawbreakers, gave the
district a welcome respite.

When John Norden had completed his survey of the Manor,
King James decided to bestow it on his son, Charles, Prince of
Wales. In theory the Lord still held the freedoms that had
belonged to Syon, including the right to execute criminals, but
there is no evidence of Norwood having ever employed his
gallows, in spite of his quarrelsome love of litigation. The Lord's
powers had declined through disuse. The Manor now comprised 223 tenancies of various types and a class of landless men
was arising. On the other hand some prosperous freeholders had
grown into considerable landowners. Norden's Survey led to
the Cheltenham Manor Act of 1625 which defined the connection of the Lord with his various types of tenant. It was to prove
of value to future generations for it simplified the conditions of
tenancy, sale and inheritance, and gave tenants such protection
in cases of dispute 'that the copyholder has invariably gained
the victory'. It included one most unusual provision for the
period – that no copyholder could sell without his wife's consent.
Three years later, when the Prince of Wales succeeded as
Charles I, he decided to sell the Manor outright. The new
owner was John Dutton of Sherborne, who paid £1200 for the
Lordship, and with this sale Cheltenham's long connection
with the Crown came to an end.

'Crump' Dutton, as the new Lord of the Manor was called,
because he was a hunchback, was described as 'a learned
prudent man and as one of the richest, so one of the meekest
men in England'. The 'prudence' hardly squares with a story of
his youth, that when he inherited Sherborne he promptly
pledged it as a stake at a gambling party. He was only re-
strained by his butler, who, overhearing the wager, bore him
forcibly away and locked him up till his guests had gone home.
He was thirty-five when he came into possession of Cheltenham
Manor, and owned so much property that he could ride from
there to Sherborne without his horse putting a hoof on any-

body else's land. Sherborne (not the one in Dorset) was a sheep-shearing centre sixteen miles from Cheltenham between North-leach and Burford and had originally belonged to the monks of Winchcombe. Dutton was a B.A. of Oxford, a member of the Middle Temple and Member of Parliament for Gloucester from 1625. He was a man of independent ideas who began as a Royalist but was converted to the Parliamentary faction after the Civil War, ending, surprisingly, as a valued friend of the Lord Protector. The epitaph in Sherborne church, under a standing effigy wrapped in a shroud reminiscent of that of John Donne in St Paul's, describes 'a person of sharp understanding and clear judgment . . . one who was a master of a large fortune and owner of a mind equal to it; noted for his great hospitality farr and neer and his charitable relief to the poor'.

Cheltenham had come under Puritan influence by the time of the Manor sale. The Church House, formerly used for parish jollifications, had been leased to respectable elderly poor and no longer resounded with merry laughter on the festivals of the Christian year. The same could not be said for Charlton Kings where, to the scandal of some, there continued to be 'Maypoles on Whit Sunday, and Church Ales on the Lord's day with dancing in time of prayer'. The Puritan influence came from Gloucester where Miles Smith was Bishop. With the appoint-ment of William, later Archbishop, Laud, as Dean in 1616, the higher forms of worship began to creep back. In his year of office Laud repaired the fabric of the cathedral and in so doing had the communion table restored from the crossing to the east end. His influence spread locally and the next Bishop, Good-man, was practically a Roman Catholic. When Goodman was arrested at the same time as Laud, Cheltenham's incumbent, Dr English, was one of his adherents who suffered at Puritan hands, being gaoled for eighteen weeks. The following inscrip-tion can still be read on the walls of the parish church –

The sad memoriall of John English, Dr in Divinitie,
to Jane, his most deare wife, davghter of the H^{le}
Elizth, Lady Sandys, Baroness de la Vine, Comit, Southton,
from whom hee was divorced by 18 weeks close imprisonm^{t},
which soone cavsed her death on Avg: 8th, 1643;
& to Marie, his 2^{d} davghter, who deceased Octr 25 followin.

'Crump' Dutton, reputed to have been in prison for refusing to pay Charles I's Ship Money, was certainly put there at another time for declining to collect forced loans from his tenants. But in 1640 he sat with the Long Parliament, unhappy at the extreme Puritanism of some of his fellow members. Cheltenham was still predominantly Royalist when the Civil War broke out. Apart from the Lord of the Manor, Henry Norwood, grandson of the former Lord, and John Stubbes, the Attorney, were on the royal side. The owners of the nearby castles of Berkeley and Sudeley were King's men, as was Sir Baptist Hicks, who went to the length of burning his new £30,000 mansion at Campden to save it from the Roundheads – a futile gesture as the Parliamentary troops never entered that town. Bristol and Cirencester and nearby Gloucester, however, were strongly Parliamentarian. The first real battle of the war had been fought at Edgehill in 1642 on the north-east extremity of the Cotswolds, where the Roundhead leader, the Earl of Essex, had an indecisive encounter with Prince Rupert. It was not till the next summer that the war moved near to Cheltenham again, when Charles's Queen entered Stratford-upon-Avon in July with 4000 troops. She spent the night in Shakespeare's house, then in the possession of his daughter, Mrs Hall. Two days later she joined the King and went to Oxford, where John Dutton had gone when London became too hot for many Royalists – 'being frightened thence by tumults which came up to the Parliament door'. Bristol had surrendered to Prince Rupert, but London was in turmoil. With most of his adherents in Oxford, the King, misled by their divided counsels, lost his best chance to march on the capital and put a speedy end to the war. No really powerful man had yet emerged to lead the Parliamentary armies.

The King's troops now held most of the north as well as Bristol, Plymouth and Tewkesbury, but the Puritan stronghold of Gloucester barred the passage of the Severn between the two areas. Charles resolved to capture this city. There were 5000 inhabitants and a Roundhead garrison of 1500 under Colonel Edward Massey. The entire Gloucester population organized itself for siege, setting fire to the houses outside its walls and employing women and children to plug up breaches in the fortifications made by enemy gunfire. They held out for nearly a month. Meantime the Earl of Essex marched west at the head of 15,000 Roundheads, raised with difficulty in London and including the London train-bands. They met with little opposition beyond a brief skirmish with Rupert near Stow-on-the-Wold. Essex arrived on Cleeve Hill in a typical Cheltenham downpour, and while the infantry slid muddily down into Prestbury, the rearguard had to spend the night on the hills in so severe a storm that 'divers of their horses died'. Essex fired four salvos of ordnance from Cleeve to encourage the people of Gloucester with the promise that help was at hand.

> The next morning our soldiers came down from Prestbury Hill into the village, being wet to the skin, but could get little or no refreshing, every house being so full of soldiers; the cavaliers were in the town but the day before. We staid here but two or three hours that morning: our soldiers began to complain pitifully, being even worn out, quite spent for want of some refreshing, some complaining that they had not eat nor drank for two days, some longer time.

Alarmed at the sound of cannon from the hills, the King sent pacific messages to Essex, but was met with the reply that he had no commission to parley 'but to relieve Gloucester; I will do it, or leave my body beneath its walls'. Essex marched into the city, arriving at the moment when the brave and famished citizens were down to their last two kegs of gunpowder. The King led his troops sadly towards Winchcombe, where he was sheltered in Sudeley Castle by its owner, Lord Chandos.

With Gloucester freed the war moved south. Essex led his motley army 'taken from the loom and the anvil, from the shops of Ludgate and the wharfs of Billingsgate' to Cirencester, and by arriving when the Royalists were fast asleep was able to help himself to all the stores he needed. He went on to fight at Newbury, where, though neither side gained a victory, the train-bands proved they had been disciplined into efficient professional soldiers. The battle was indecisive, but Charles lost his final chance to regain London.

Cheltenham had one further brush with the opposing armies

when Colonel Massey, now short of money and supplies, decided to raid it and help himself to the rents due to the dispossessed Lord of the Manor. Hearing of this, Lord Chandos rode over from Sudeley with a small army, defeated the raiders and returned home unscathed. From then on Cheltenham was left in peace.

It was after this final phase of the war, the peace terms of which he is reputed to have drafted, that Dutton, who had never wholly seen eye to eye with the King, seems to have come round to the Puritan way of thinking. A rich man, he was willing to pay Parliament the heavy fine demanded for the return of his estates – £2216 – and Cromwell gave him permission to hunt in Wychwood and take deer from there to restock Sherborne Park. It was at this time that he formed his intimacy with the Lord Protector, who had now emerged as leader of the Roundhead party. Dutton's conversion was so complete that he disinherited his own grandchildren because his daughter had helped to shelter the King at Coberley, and left his lands to his nephew William. Young Dutton was sent to be educated in the Cromwell household, where he was tutored by the poet Andrew Marvell. His uncle's hope, that he might marry Oliver's daughter, Frances, came to nothing, for that beautiful young woman had set her heart on someone else.

Among other Cheltenham worthies, Stubbes, who lent £20 to Charles I in a moment of crisis, and Henry Norwood of Leckhampton, remained Royalist. The former was too old for much involvement, but Norwood fled to Holland and went from thence to join his cousin Sir William Berkeley, the Governor of Virginia. Norwood's chief claim to remembrance is his book, *Voyage to Virginia*, which described the shipwreck, starvation and other horrors of that journey. After the Restoration, and a spell as Governor of Tangier, he returned to Leckhampton and ended as Member of Parliament for Gloucester and Mayor of that city.

The melancholy Dr English returned to the parish church after his release from prison, but was eventually removed from office on the pretext that he held other benefices, contrary to the agreement with Jesus College. The Church was in a ferment as a result of the Commonwealth's attempt to reform its services to reward the Presbyterian Scots for their help in the war. The new ministers were Puritan, but Dr English, who died a year after his sequestration, was permitted to be buried in Cheltenham near the sad memorial to his wife and daughter. The 'able preaching minister' appointed at the end of the wars was John Cooper, who estimated that he had 350 families in his cure of souls.

During all this time, taking advantage of the national turmoil, the local farmers had been planting their tobacco undisturbed and passing it off as the genuine West Indian article, but with the peace complaints from Bristol again began to pour in. By 1652 Parliament had time at last to deal with lesser lawbreakers and a new Act was passed in April of that year against illegal growers, followed in May by 'the humble petition and cries of many land owners and labourers of Cheltenham and Winchcombe' against the removal of their chief source of profit. It was then agreed that the farmers might have a year's grace to harvest fields already planted, but that after that they must revert to indigenous crops. Six years later, however, 'ye weed called tobacco' was still flourishing in 'ye common fields' of Gloucester and Parliament despatched one Cornet Joyce with a party of horse, who set about to destroy the plants. He was met with a well-organized opposition of five or six hundred 'men and women, calling out for blood for the tobacco', threatening to kill them, both horses and men, and they had to beat an ignominious retreat. One of the party sent to destroy the crops, wrote, 'Ten men could not in four days destroy the good tobacco about Cheltenham. The cornet would not act, and some of the country troops are dealers and planters. I was forced to retreat. The Justices of the Peace rather hinder than help us. The soldiers say, if this be suffered, farewell the Virginia trade for tobacco.'

It was at least another thirty years before local growers gave up their illegal practice, for Pepys recorded attempts by the Life Guards and other bodies to invade the farms and uproot the crops. Cheltenham farmers felt safe to take risks so long as profits remained high. Communications depended on only one decent road which ran from Winchcombe to Gloucester by way of Swindon village, skirting the north of the town at the present suburb of Prestbury. The nefarious practice ended, not through any action of authority, but because of a slump in the price of Virginia tobacco, which made the crop not worth the danger its growing entailed. Cheltenham had other resources in its market and its brewing and did not suffer so much distress as Winchcombe by the ending of the trade.

CHAPTER FIVE

Skillicorne's Spring

IF any town ought to leave its pigeon pests in peace it is Cheltenham. To these unwelcomed birds, the legend says, it owes the beginning of its fame, and two pigeons stand proudly in its coat of arms in recognition of their part in its rise to prosperity. A quarter of a mile south-west of the parish church, across the Chelt and up the gentle slope of Bayshill, a little spring gushed through the clay and, drying in the sun, left a deposit of salt. In about 1716 the pigeons drew attention to this phenomenon when they were noticed gathering in flocks to peck the glittering crystals. The spring rose in a field belonging to a Quaker, William Mason. Certain old men apparently knew as much as the birds about the medicinal properties of the water, for Dr Lucas, who later analysed it, had seen them downing it by the quart without 'experiencing any ill effect from so strange a practice'. Some had drunk it for 'upwards of thirty years without having any disorder, but because they thought it wholesome to cleanse their bodies; therefore observed no rule but to drink till the water passed clean through them'. Elegant society was beginning to gather at Bath, Tunbridge Wells, Scarborough and Clifton to drink mineral waters and it was not long before the rumour of an efficacious spring at Cheltenham made it necessary for Mason to have it 'railed in, locked up, and a little shed thrown over it'. For a time it was principally distributed in bottles, reaching as far as London. A good deal of the water so labelled is thought to have been spurious. It is to be hoped it did not harm its distant buyers and that the 'old men' locally did not suffer too greatly from the summary cutting off of their free supply. The precise location of the spring is not known. It is probably buried underneath the Princess Hall, that remarkable Victorian erection in the Ladies' College.

The little parish that was to become so fashionable a watering-place had been described by John Prinn, Steward to the Duttons and Lord of Ashley Manor in Charlton, shortly before its rise to fame – 'situated on the eastern side of one of the most fertile valleys in ye world, and an ancient Market Town. . . . Its soil is sandy and very natural for carrots, cabbages and turnips – insomuch as the whole neighbourhood is annually furnished with these for sundry miles around.' Prinn shared John Stubbes's passion for collecting local records and it is to these two stewards that posterity owes most of its knowledge of Cheltenham before it rose to be a spa. Sir Robert Atkyns, in his *History of Gloucestershire*, published about the time of the spring's discovery, counted 321 houses with about 1500 living in them. About thirty-five years earlier a religious census listed 1068 communicants at the parish church, 97 nonconformists and 4 papists. It did not specify the sects of the 97, but William Mason's, the Quakers, had been meeting in secret since 1670 and legally since 1689. By 1696 there were sufficient of them for the building of a Friends' Meeting House, the first dissenting chapel in Cheltenham. Not long after, the Anabaptists also erected one.

Little had been done to the parish church since the Reformation beyond increasing the original two bells to a peal of eight. It held a small charity school 'for teaching poor children to write', to attend which thirty boys in costumes reminiscent of Christ's Hospital – long coats, yellow stockings, bands and caps – daily climbed the narrow stair into the little room over the north porch, and at one point in their history had to carry their aged schoolmaster pick-a-back with them. Richard Pate's Elizabethan building, already venerable, with 'Scola Grammatica' roughly carved on its frontage, stood to the north of the church. The Fleece Inn and the chapels were at this end of the Street, with the old Court House, sold to a private owner and shortly to be pulled down. Going east from the beautiful spire, the Street continued past the old Booth Hall, used as a market hall, and the prison, known as the 'Blind House', to the principal Market House, a free-standing building on stone piles which had replaced the one which fell into dilapidation at the time of the Civil War and above which the Court Leets were held. Pate's other foundation stood opposite the present Rodney Road – 'a large antique body – with a chapel attached, where a pendant bell indicated that the solemn rites of religious worship are celebrated within its hallowed walls. A green-sward ornaments the front, and following the path upwards to the doorway on a sunken tablet of stone . . . this inscription "Alms Houses of the Holy and Indivisible Trinity".' This was the pleasant home where six old people lived, having 'everyone of them a private chamber . . . and a private garden at the backside thereof . . . and the pasture and profit of the orchard and close'. Each Friday they received a shilling, with an extra fourpence quarterly and seven yards of black frieze for their clothing, a provision more than adequate by the standards of the time. Rodney Road was then a lane with a good-sized house known as Powers Court on the church side and, on the other, Cambray Meadow with the Parsonage House and the farm and the ruins of the Saxon priory by the Mill. The town boasted other inns beside the Plough and the Fleece, including the Swan and the Crown.

Down the middle of the Street, nowadays a congested, un-designed double row of chain stores and supermarkets, violets and primroses grew between thatched cottages, and horses cropped the grass on either side of the diverted stream. This ran, to a greater or lesser degree, according to the day of the week or the disposition of the millers. Stepping-stones enabled people to cross, and on days of street cleansing an unwary pedestrian could slip into the water up to the knee. In summer, in drought, or when the millers shirked their duty, the water declined to a muddy trickle and was the cause of odours offensive to the nostrils of the elegant visitors who began to arrive in quest of the waters. At the time of their discovery the Court Books were still recording arguments about the cleaning of the Street. The stocks and the whipping-post were still in use, the former for profanity or haunting ale-houses with lewd women; the latter for hedge-breaking, the theft of wood or other property. These offences were now the province of the Justice of the Peace, while serious crime was tried at the Quarter Sessions. The power of the Manor continued to decline, most people preferring to pay a fine rather than attend its half-yearly courts.

William Mason, in whose field the spring had been discovered, retired to Bristol, where his daughter met a merchant seaman called Henry Skillicorne. Captain Skillicorne was a Manxman and a widower. He married Elizabeth Mason and moved to Cheltenham when, in 1738, she inherited her father's property on Bayshill. Skillicorne may be said to be the father of Cheltenham Spa. He is also the owner of the longest epitaph in Britain – 587 words on a tablet in the parish church which give his biography and character, the pedigrees of his wives and a detailed history of the development of the Spa. According to this instructive stone document, 'he found the Old Spring open and exposed to the weather', suggesting that Mason's little shed had been allowed to fall down.

The Captain knew the hot wells of Clifton, where there was a simple pump-room, and he quickly saw the possibilities of Mason's spring. Without wasting a moment he had it covered with a shelter – a canopy supported on four brick arches with the pigeons at each corner – had it deepened and installed a pumping system. The next year he turned his attention to making an approach from the town and was assisted in this project by a member of the family from Berkeley Castle, Narbonne Berkeley, Lord Botetourt, who helped design the Well Walk. In accordance with the garden-planning fashionable at the period it was to be a rural vista, a double avenue of elms and limes from the well down to the river, and continuing over a rustic bridge across Church Meadow. From the bridge the visitor could look up Bayshill to the Pump Room, while to the north the trees would frame the slender spire. The owner of the Meadow would not agree to this plan, so the avenue had to stop short of the church, the walk ending in a winding gravel path over the last few hundred yards. The waters, analysed in 1721, were given fresh publicity in Dr Short's *History of Mineral Waters* in 1740, where the claim that they were the most efficacious in the country gave a boost to the Captain's plans. Skillicorne wrote of his progress, of his setbacks, and of the immediate success and quickly increasing patronage of his well.

> In the winter of 1739 I made the upper walk, planted elms and limes to the number of 37, and made a new orchard adjoining. The winter 1740 I made the lower walk, planted 96 elms, at the expense of £56. Had that summer 414 subscribers at the Wells at 12d per piece. Built a yard round it, and 18 little houses. The summer 1740 proving very dry, I had 46 of the trees dead; set 44 in the room of the 46 dead the summer before, and had that summer 674 subscribers at the Wells at 12d per piece. The summer 1741, proving very dry, 30 trees dead . . . which I planted again. Had this season 667 subscribers.

Beautiful old trees are still one of Cheltenham's principal glories, but it is unlikely that any of the Captain's still stand. Some people believe that several ancient planes in the Royal Crescent bus station could be part of the original avenue, but these do not seem to fit in with the scheme of 1740. The straight line of Well Walk is now obliterated. From the church along the present Royal Well Walk it would have crossed the now invisible Chelt near the east end of St George's Road and disappeared into the mass of buildings that makes up the Ladies' College, running parallel to the Promenade on the west.

On the left of the walk, as the visitor returned from drinking the waters, stood the newly constructed Grove House, on the site of the old Court House and the present St Matthew's Church. Here he might turn aside for entertainment in the form of cards or dancing. Popularly known as Mrs Field's Boarding House, it was the principal place of resort apart from the Pump Room.

The waters were composed of 'muriate of soda, sulphates of soda, lime and magnesia, oxide of iron, chloride of magnesium, and iodine and bromide', and cures were claimed for almost every ailment known to eighteenth-century man. The Cheltenham *Guides* described their action as 'a most commodious purge for those who do not bear strong cathartics' which 'works off without heat, thirst, or dryness of the mouth, sickness, gripings,

faintness or dejection of spirits; but rather increases the appetite, and strengthens the stomach'. They were effective in 'all
bilious complaints, obstructions of the liver and spleen,
obstructed perspiration, loss of appetite, bad digestion, and all
disorders of the primae viae'; they restored 'a relaxed habit,
whether from long residence in a hot climate, free living, use of
mercurials, or any other cause' and were of benefit in 'rheu-
matic, scrophulous, erysipelous, scorbutic, leprous cases'. One
particular property was to have a profound effect on the future
of the town – 'the benefit derived by many just returned from
the East Indies in a debilitated state'. Some doctors thought
the water unsuited to people with 'weak nerves, paralytic,
hypocondriac, or hysteric disorders, or to those who are subject
to any kinds of fits, cramps or convulsions', but those whose
interest was to advertise the Wells begged leave to differ from
their opinion.

The entertainment offered locally was unsophisticated and,
cock fighting apart, cannot have appealed greatly to the gentry.
There were cudgel matches on a stage at the Plough – 'he that
breaks the most heads in three bouts, and comes off clear, to
receive a good hat, and a guinea in money; the second best
player, half a guinea; and every person whose head is broken,
1 shilling. . . . Betwixt the hours of 10 and 2, there will be a
gown jigged for by the girls.' The ladies did not like the High
Street, soiling their gowns on the muddy stepping-stones. They
stigmatized the rivulet as an open sewer. It was difficult to
progress along either side of it, even where roughly paved, for
the accumulation of obstacles – cattle and horses with their
inevitable nuisance; wheelbarrows, casks and other impedi-
menta of the brewing trade; the peasantry letting off their high
spirits in 'football, cockthrowing, bullbaiting' round every
corner, or in the 'release of squibs, serpents, rockets and fireworks' in an indiscriminate manner – sometimes, perhaps,
deliberately to annoy their fine new tourists. The pillared
Market Hall, the Cross, the ancient alms-houses drew sneers
from the quality, but above all it was the lack of decent accommodation and the notable absence of hospitality that offended
them. Few of the natives shared the enthusiasm of the Manx

Skillicorne and his successors – his son, William, and two 'foreigners' from London and Wales – for making the town a place of resort for the wealthy.

To combat this unfortunate reputation the Gloucestershire and London press for some years published this advertisement:

> Whereas the famous purging mineral waters at Cheltenham
> ... have not been for some years past, so much resorted to as
> formerly, from a report that the inhabitants of the said town
> were exorbitant in their demands, and no convenience to be
> had reasonably: By an unanimous meeting, consent, and
> agreement of the gentlemen, tradesmen, and innholders of the
> said town: This is to certify that all gentlemen, ladies and
> others may meet with kind reception and good usage, with
> convenient lodgings and ordinances kept, if encouraged, at
> reasonable rates.

Ten years after its promising beginning the Spa's popularity was falling off, despite visits from such celebrities as Handel and Dr Johnson, for Thomas Hughes, who leased the well from the ageing Skillicorne, was exempted in 1757 from paying rates on the property. Smallpox kept people away for some years. Some were deterred by the difficulty of the journey. The only London coach that came near advertised in these terms: 'If God permitted', the Gloucester Flying Machine would perform its journey 'in the short space of three days'. It entailed a change at Andoversford or the hiring of a private carriage from Gloucester. By the 1770s the town, which had begun to improve with the making of the Well Walk, had relapsed into its former state of neglect.

Captain Skillicorne died in 1763. He was eighty-four. His epitaph which describes him first as being 'tall, erect, robust and active' goes on to say 'from an ill treated wound, while a prisoner, after an engagement at sea, he became a strict valetudinarian'. It chronicles his character and past exploits.

> He was an excellent seaman of tried courage. He visited most
> of the great trading ports of the Mediterranean, up the
> Archipelago, Morea, Turkey, Spain, Portugal and Venice,
> and several of the North African ports, Philadelphia, and
> Boston, and Holland, and could do business in seven tongues.
> He was of great regularity and probity, and so temperate a

man as never to have been once intoxicated. Religious without hypocrisy, grave without austerity, of a cheerful conversation without levity, a kind and tender father. . . . He lived and dyed an honest man.

He was buried near the west door inside the parish church, but he permitted his wife, Elizabeth Mason, who survived him sixteen years, to continue in her father's persuasion. His memorial records that she was buried in the Quakers' Graveyard.

Cheltenham was still one long street with the charming right-angled extension of Skillicorne's walk, its trees now well grown, when, in the early 1770s, it began again to rise in fame and amenity. Communications and lodgings improved to a small degree.

There were two good inns, at both of which in the season a few families and individuals took up temporary residence. Our stage coach, the 'Old Hereford' which, with six horses, accomplished the journey to London in twenty-six hours, astounded the inhabitants by the celerity of its movement. Few of them, however, aspired to the honour of visiting the Metropolis in a coach, and those who did contented themselves with a place in an enormous basket which was attached to the hinder part of the body.

The founders of the new Cheltenham were William, Captain Skillicorne's son, and the 'foreigners' William Miller, a Londoner, who became his partner at the Well, and Thomas Hughes, from Monmouthshire, who was to build the first Assembly Rooms.

No proper theatre had been built, but travelling companies presented plays in a fitted-up malthouse, 'a poor place, little better than a barn' in what is now Pittville Street. There were few evening entertainments and it was well patronized. An engagement to act there proved to be the turning-point for the recently married Mr and Mrs Siddons. It happened that the Honourable Mrs Boyle, 'authoress of several pleasing poems', was staying in the town in 1774 with her stepfather, the Earl of Aylesbury. Early in the day they went to the box office to find out what treat was in store for the evening and when they discovered Otway's *Venice Preserv'd* on the bill 'they all laughed heartily and promised themselves a treat of the ludicrous'. Their conversation was unkindly reported to the young actress who was to play Belvediera. The future Queen of the English Stage made her entrance alarmed and mortified, struggled through her part and, thinking she had heard suppressed mirth among the audience, went home in tears. She was not the only one. Next morning Lord Aylesbury ran into Mr Siddons in the street and not only expressed his admiration of the performance, but described its effect on his lady companions. 'They had wept, he said, so excessively, that they were unpresentable in the morning, and were confined to their rooms with headaches.' Mr Siddons bore the good news to his wife and her next caller was Mrs Boyle herself. It was she who used her influence to bring the actress to Garrick's notice, and, not long after, Sarah Siddons was playing in London.

A visitor with a different purpose, in the days immediately before the Spa's second rise to fame, was the evangelist John Wesley, who came in the spring of 1766. He could not find a room to hold the crowd that gathered to hear him and was forced to preach in the open air in a 'piercing northeast wind'. In spite of this, none of his congregation, 'rich or poor', left before he had concluded. He was back in the autumn, again in cold weather, but this time was able to acquire the chapel for his sermon and was pleased to find his followers full of lively belief and 'quite free from the bigotry which is common in Cheltenham'. Two years later he returned and managed to address his growing flock in comfort – 'though it would not have been so if either the Rector or the Anabaptist minister could have prevented it. Both these have blown the trumpet with their might, but the public have no ears to hear them.'

Young Skillicorne and Miller opened a new Long Room at the Well. In its first season of 1776 visitors were increasing. By 1780, when Thomas Hughes was building the first Assembly Rooms, a new character had appeared in the walks – one Simon Moreau, described by the Honourable John Byng as having been *arbiter elegantiarum* at Bath. Moreau's determination to be crowned in a similar role for Cheltenham earned him the hostility of those who looked upon themselves as reigning there already – particularly Miller and Mrs Field. Byng stayed at Mrs Field's in June 1781 and kept a diary of the daily life of the Spa, the more lively because he disliked the place so much, and of the struggle for supremacy between Miller and Moreau. 'This place, like all others, is divided into two factions; the greater and more powerful party . . . are averse from a master of the ceremonies in the person of Mr Moreau, supported by Mrs Jones of the Town Rooms, and the generality of the company; – I have heard both parties, and neither liking the character and manners of my hostess, am inclined to yield subjection to Mr Moreau, who, to be sure, is only self-elected.'

Byng had arrived at the Swan, but moved next day to Mrs Field's, which was nearer to the Well and more convenient for his wife's bad legs. His first impression of Grove House was favourable – 'comfortable, neat and spacious . . . and over-looking lovely meadows' – but the lodgings did not provide food, and the necessity of procuring and cooking their own and the high prices charged in the town (salmon at sevenpence or eightpence a pound) quickly altered his views. 'Our company are a scurvy set. . . . I already begin to dislike Cheltenham and principally for the dearness of every article which is equal to the most polish'd places of publick entertainment.' He approved the shady walks but not the 'band of fiddles' hired 'to assist with their musick the operation of the waters', for Byng was one of those who dislike to have music forced upon them, 'whether the opera band or Bach's concerts', preferring to choose his time of attention and distance from it. He did not object to its use at public breakfasts, held in the Long Room every Monday at a shilling a head; 'there is a gaiety in a publick breakfast in a summer's morning, with musick, that is to me very pleasing, every one then looks fresh and happy; the women are in their natural looks, not disfigured by over dress and paint, and the men are civil and sober'. In June there were about eighty people, 'but at the full of the season the number amounts to 200 or 300'. Water-drinking began early in the day, while the fiddles played from eight o'clock until ten. From then till three o'clock Byng passed his time exploring the country. Another

Cheltenham old and new: above *taking the air on the Promenade;* below *the new shopping-centre at Coronation Square.*

The Plough Hotel was already in existence before the seventeenth century and still stands, its bars and restaurants crowded, in the High Street, looking much as it did in the early nineteenth century.

The Parish Church of St Mary. First built in the twelfth century, probably on Saxon foundations, it was enlarged in the fourteenth century when the spire, 167 feet high, was also added. In the churchyard is the cross beside which John Wesley preached.

Bayshill Lodge, built in 1781 by Lord Fauconberg 'two small fields and an orchard away from the Old Well' and originally known as Fauconberg House. In 1788 it was lent for George III's visit.

View of the town of Cheltenham in about 1825 looking south from Marle Hill. Holy Trinity Church is in the middle, the spire of the Parish Church between the trees on the right.

Above left: *Captain Skillicorne, Manx sea-captain, founder of Cheltenham Spa and owner of the longest epitaph in any church in the British Isles.*

Right: *The Reverend Francis Close, first a curate at Holy Trinity and later Perpetual Curate of the Parish Church. Opponent of railways, racing, theatres and all forms of entertainment, he was the greatest power in the town and was described by Tennyson as Cheltenham's Pope. He was also the founder or inspirer of most of the town's many schools and training colleges. He later became Dean of Carlisle.*

King George III drinking his morning glass of Cheltenham water under the little brick canopy put over the original well by Captain Skillicorne. The King, Queen, and two of their daughters spent five weeks in Cheltenham in 1788.

Two views of Skillicorne's Well Walk, the one looking towards the ancient parish church of St Mary; the other, including the rustic bridge over the Chelt, towards the original Pump Room.

The Centenary Fête of the Royal Old Well Walk in August 1838.

The Prince Regent (Mr John Jeens) with Mrs Fitzherbert (Mrs Ann Foster) and Alderman Aimbury Dodwell, Chairman of the British Spas Federation and of Cheltenham Entertainments Committee, drinking the first sample from the new well at the Pittville Pump Room during the 1970 Regency Rout.

Joseph Pitt's great Pump Room seen from across the ornamental lake in his park. The progress of the building was watched daily by the Duke of Wellington on his 1825 visit, when he talked with workmen who had fought at Waterloo.

The partly restored Pittville Pump Room. The building was occupied by the American Forces of Supply during the Second World War when dry rot was allowed to spread unchecked. It has now been miraculously restored by public subscription, inside and out, and was finally reopened by the 8th Duke of Wellington. The picture shows it uncompleted, without the statues of Hygeia, Hippocrates and Aesculapius, which have now been added by sculptors from Boulton's workshop.

The restored central dome in the ballroom of the Pittville Pump Room.

The Sherborne Pump Room, later known as the Imperial Spa, was the first of Cheltenham's many buildings modelled on the Greek Temple of Illyssus. Though it lasted for a shorter time than any of the other pump rooms it was the most important for the town's development, because the Promenade was created as an avenue to lead to it from the High Street. Where it once stood is now the site of the Queens Hotel. The statue on its roof is Cheltenham's presiding deity – the goddess Hygeia.

hour was spent at the Well in the evening, and the visitors usually went to bed early after 'some slight repast'. Monday and Thursday were ball nights, beginning in early June; the players from Tewkesbury were opening at the theatre. Cards and tea was to be had at Mrs Field's or at Mrs Jones's (the Old Room) behind the Plough. There was a farm called The Gallipot on the hill above the Well 'to which parties are made for tea, syllabub, etc.'

The season of 1781 started damply, a thing not unusual under Cleeve Hill, and a fact which may have aggravated the tempers of the contestants for power. 'It should never rain at a public place,' concluded Byng, 'as it prevents intercourse, and drives everyone to his own bad lodging to breed spleen and ennui. The first publick meeting of the season was held last night at Mrs Jones's rooms, where was sufficient company to form six couple of dancers, and one card table.' He condescended to enjoy a game of whist, at which he amused himself by taking £2 10s 6d off the Reverend Hugh Hughes, 'whose stipend is forty pounds per annum'. He noted, however, that the Perpetual Curate was generally able to augment this meagre wage by his skill at the game. Divine Service on Sundays was 'as irreligiously performed here, as at most other places', a fact which Byng attributed to a want of discipline in the Church of England which sent people flying for spiritual comfort to Wesley and to other persuasions.

The weather was occasionally fine enough to permit the visitor to make some pleasant rides, between the waters and dinner, along lanes which, with the exception of the London road through Leckhampton, were uniformly dirty. Byng observed the remains of Roman camps, 'several of them unhurt by the plough', went to look at Belas Knapp and the ruins of Sudeley Castle. To his way of thinking, the best house in Cheltenham was that of the Steward, John de la Bere, which stood in the High Street next to the Almshouse on the site now occupied by Woolworths. He admired Mr Prinn's 'neat house' with its small deer park at Charlton Kings. Lord Fauconberg arrived with his family at Mrs Field's, 'which frights the house from its propriety', and struck up a friendship with Byng, and on several mornings Byng went up Bayshill to watch bricks being baked in a kiln and foundations dug for the mansion Skillicorne was erecting for the Lord. 'It will be pleasantly placed, two fields from the pump, and will command agreeable views.' Byng did his best to avert a folly, which, if he had succeeded, would have earned him blessings from many a domestic – 'I endeavoured to persuade Lord Fauconberg from building his kitchen under the house; for which there can be no reason in the country.' He was not heeded, and the house, which was to become famous by the end of the decade, was set incongruously on a half basement. Byng's greatest pleasure, when the weather was dry, was in 'walks at the back of the town through meadows and by the banks of the trout stream . . . particularly now, being the hay season', and riding in the Marsh 'which is the Rotten Row of the place and has pleasing views of the hills'. But the life of the Spa disgusted him.

> After some stay in one of these places, there is nothing left to see, say or do; and that is the case at the present with me, for my life passes in the dullest gloom: at one's own home there is allways something to amuse, but in these places I soon lose my happiness and retain only noise and unsettledness.

For all his boredom, Byng was not simply an observer, but took some part in the quarrel for supremacy between Miller and the would-be Beau from Bath.

> Mr Miller of the Long Room continued his impertinence and tyranny to Mr and Mrs Moreau by refusing them the waters (tho' Mrs C's mangy dog drank of it constantly). . . . After dinner, at the Walks this affair was canvas'd and some gentlemen meeting in Mrs Field's room . . . sent to Mr Miller, who return'd this polite answer, 'That anyone who wanted him, might call on him'. Accordingly – a deputation of four gentlemen waited upon the great man, who at first was very violent, refused to have connection with Moreau etc. etc; but at last all was compromised, and by shaking of hands, a kind of peace was established: Poor Moreau was in agonies of joy, and at his return home, fell into hysteric fits.

Byng departed on 27 June, summing up his feelings at saying goodbye to the new Spa in the following words –

Cheltenham I quit thee with pleasure, and hope never to revisit thee! I believe I may aver, to be agreed with, that Cheltenham is the dullest of publick places; the look of the place is sombre, the lodgings dear and pitiful, and no inns or stabling fit for the reception of gentlemen, or their horses.

CHAPTER SIX

A Good Sort of Man

BUT Byng did revisit Cheltenham. He came back in another downpour two years later and was perversely sorry to see that the place he so disliked had been altered.

> Since my visit new rooms are built; and likewise a new theatre; what served our ancestors won't do now. We substitute taste, and fashion for substantial comforts, and by these improvements every thing becomes dear, and formal; and people do not live at these places upon the familiar footing as heretofore; but league together according to their dignity; thus it happens that discontents arise from punctilio, and a neglect of card leaving occasions eternal shyness!!

The place was full of 'widows wanting husbands, old men wanting health, and misses wanting partners'.

The rift between Miller and the upstart from Bath had evidently been healed, but a doggerel verse, locally published and probably inspired by Mrs Field, expressed something of the same sentiments as Byng.

> In short, I'm unable our pleasure to draw
> Good breeding and sense were our guide and our law,
> Without form we were gay – good humour went round,
> And Mirth with Contentment, Society crowned;
> But lately an ape in the form of a Beau
> By the outlandish name of Simon Moreau
> Has officially come at the balls to preside,
> To preserve etiquette, and pay homage to Pride.
> Some use there may be in this creature 'tis true
> Their way to the temple the ladies to shew;
> But I still must lament that such forms should efface
> The native politeness and ease of the place.

Moreau by now was securely enthroned Master of Ceremonies and had taken over the editorship of the *Cheltenham
Guide* which had made its first appearance in 1781. According
to this life at the Spa was continuing much as before, with a
five-shilling subscription to the Pump Room, Monday breakfasts and evening balls at a shilling. There was no need to dress
for the Monday ball, 'no public place being so free from
restraints as this'. A circulating library had opened in the High
Street at five shillings a season, and Mr Harward's 'neat and
commodious' shop where harpsichords could be rented. As Byng
noted, the rustic barn where Mrs Siddons had played Otway
was replaced by a 'very pretty little theatre' built north of the
High Street opposite Cambray by John Boles Watson, himself
a touring actor. The principal change was in the acquisition of
new Assembly Rooms put up by Thomas Hughes, who had
stepped into Moreau's shoes as Miller's chief antagonist.
Hughes, once a clerk in John de la Bere's office, had married a
local heiress. With the backing of her fortune he set up his own
legal practice and bought Powers Court with its estate stretching
south along Rodney Road to the present Oriel Terrace. His
new building was on the site of Mrs Jones's old rooms. The
dimensions, 60 feet by 30 feet, were about the same as Miller's
Room at the Well, but the interior was more elegant, with
Corinthian pilasters, chandeliers and lustres, and a small
gallery for the musicians. It proved a serious rival to the Well
ballroom, being nearer the centre of the town and the inns.

According to Moreau's *Guide*, the churchyard had been
'rendered particularly agreeable by its walks being shaded by a
double row of lime trees, which surround and cross it'. From the
Pump Room 'the church spire, rising from the centre of the
walk, forms a very pleasing point of view from the Well; on
the side opposite to which a handsome dial with a minute hand
is fixed, to the great satisfaction of the company, who had frequently expressed a desire to have one'. Skillicorne's walk, its
well-grown elms filled in between with quickset hedges,
shielded the delicate eighteenth-century complexion against
'inconvenience from sun'. Beyond the Well the narrow Serpentine Walk provided another promenade among the lime trees.

At the Pump, Mrs Hannah Forty, 'a very civil woman and a great favourite with the public' dispensed the waters which she had been pumping for the past twenty-four years. Transport was sadly inadequate, for only two sedan chairs existed and with them a condition of stalemate – few people would use them at the excessive charge of a shilling, while the owners refused to reduce the fare on the grounds that they had not sufficient custom.

The Thursday market sold local butter and poultry. Salmon, eels, gudgeon, perch, carp and tench came daily from the Severn; lobsters and crayfish twice a week from Oxford. There were sea fish from Bristol; trout from the Thames near Cirencester; Postlip Warren supplied rabbits; pigeons were shot in the nearby woods. But the market buildings still offended the eyes of the visitors and developers alike, being out of keeping with the new Assembly Rooms.

> At present the Street is greatly encumbered with certain old coarse buildings supported on stone pillars; these are called the Corn Market and Butter Cross, and another below them that neither has nor merits a name. A little further down is a kind of cage or prison built of stone, and not unsuitably decorated with an inscription in front, 'Do well and fear not'. It is to be hoped that objects so very unsightly will soon be removed.

They were. The first Act for the improvement of Cheltenham was passed in 1786, enforced by a body of Commissioners, including William Skillicorne, John de la Bere, Thomas Hughes and his son. The stone from the demolished markets was used to make a good road where the water had previously run, while this was diverted into gutters on either side of it. Foot pavements were laid, and the houses in the Street given numbers. Arrangements were made to light this decent new thoroughfare with 120 lamps.

The improvements were made just in time, though the Commissioners can hardly have guessed the publicity and glory about to descend on the town, or that two years later the nation's journals would be full of the fact that 'all fashions are completely Cheltenhamized. . . . The Cheltenham cap – the

Cheltenham bonnet – the Cheltenham buttons – the Cheltenham buckles' were being designed, sold and worn all over the country. This sudden upsurge of enthusiasm was occasioned by the visit of George III, his Queen, his daughters and a smallish entourage for the weeks between 12 July and 16 August 1788. For that short period the pages of the *Gentleman's Magazine* and *Morning Post* could speak of little else. It is not known who persuaded the King that Cheltenham water would benefit his mysterious complaint, though Moreau's *Guide* quotes Sir George Baker, one of the royal physicians, as insisting that the 'only certain way of reaping benefit from it' was to drink the water on the spot. The most intimate chronicle of that five-week holiday was made by Fanny Burney, as yet unmarried and a lady-in-waiting to Queen Charlotte. The royal family were no cowards about early rising and on the morning they set out from Windsor Fanny records:

> We were all up at five o'clock; the noise and confusion reigning through the house, and resounding all around it, from the quantities of people stirring, boxes nailing, horses neighing, and dogs barking, was tremendous.
> I must now tell you the party:
> Their Majesties; the Princesses Royal, Augusta and Elizabeth; Lady Weymouth; Mr Fairly, Colonel Gwynn, Miss Planta, and a person you have sometimes met. Pages for the King, Queen and Princesses, Wardrobe women for ditto, and footmen for all.
> A smaller party for a royal excursion cannot well be imagined. How we shall all manage Heaven knows. Miss Planta and myself are allowed no maid; the house would not hold one.

The incommodious house was Lord Fauconberg's, which John Byng had watched being built seven years before, rising somewhat incongruously from its half-basement two small fields and an orchard away from the Well, which the owner was pleased to lend for the royal convenience. The journey took ten hours, including stops for refreshment, and it seemed to Fanny that the villages all over the country had emptied themselves 'to supply all the pathways with groups of anxious spectators'.

Every town seemed all face; and all the way upon the road we rarely proceeded five miles without encountering a band of the most horrid fiddlers, scraping 'God Save the King' with all their might, out of tune, out of time, and all in the rain. . . . We arrived in Cheltenham, which is almost all one street, extremely long and clean, and well paved. . . . Fauconberg Hall . . . is indeed situated in a most sweet spot, surrounded with lofty hills beautifully variegated, and bounded, for the principal object, with the hills of Malvern.

The ladies-in-waiting were the last of the party to arrive, by which time they found the Hall surrounded by a huge crowd and the royal family already bowing to it from the windows. Making her way through the multitude proved a most 'disagreeable operation' for Fanny, who never cared to be noticed. She was at once summoned to the Queen

who was in excellent spirits, and said she would show me her room.

'*This* ma'am!' cried I, as I entered it – 'is *this* little room for your Majesty?'

'Oh stay,' cried she, laughing, 'till you see your own before you call mine little!'

. . . Mine, with one window, had just enough space to crowd in a bed, a chest of drawers, and three small chairs.

The prospect, however . . . is extremely pretty, and all is new and clean. . . . Having no maid is a real evil to one so little her own mistress as myself. I little wanted the fagging of my own clothes and dressing, to add to my daily fatigues.

The King, however, who found his way to Fanny's room while exploring his new lodgings, 'admired it prodigiously' and stayed for half an hour's chat. He found himself the only man sleeping under Lord Fauconberg's roof. His gentlemen had to be accommodated in the town, coming in for breakfast and to drink tea with the ladies, but sitting down with the King only at dinner. The house provided

one large and very pleasant room, which is made the dining-parlour. . . . A small, but very neat dressing room for His Majesty is on the other side of the hall, and my little parlour is the third and only other room on the ground floor, so you will not think our Monarch, his Consort and offspring, take up too much of the land called their own.

In spite of the inevitable downpour that greeted his arrival, and which must have damped the 'general illuminations' as well as the 'immense numbers thronged in the streets' to receive him, King George remained in excellent humour for the whole of his visit. His energy and enthusiasm both for the water cure and for exploring the rides round the town exhausted his small retinue, deprived as they were of their usual assistance. Fanny was worn out by the second day, when she went, rising again at five, to taste the water.

> I shall spare myself any further such regale, for it is not prescribed to me, and I think it very unpleasant.
> This place and the air seem very healthy; but the very early hours, and no maid! I almost doubt how this will do. The fatigue is very great indeed.

Nor did Fanny care for the famous Well Walks: 'They are straight, clay, and sided by common trees, without any rich foliage, or one beautiful opening. The meadows, and all the country round, are far preferable; yet here everybody walks.'

The royal party arrived on a Saturday, and everyone in crowded Cheltenham spent the damp evening drinking 'with plentiful though not blameable or licentious libations' toasts to the improved health of their sovereign. Either this indulgence, or awe at his Majesty's presence, inhibited the choir and congregation at St Mary's from singing heartily on the following day, and though the Bishop came from Worcester to deliver the sermon of welcome the service fell uncomfortably flat. By the next Sunday 'a very good bassoon' had been procured to support the nervous choristers, who then managed to give a lusty performance of 'How lovely are thy dwellings'. The royal party occupied three pews fitted up for them in a 'plain but neat manner'.

The King and his family were at the Wells at half past five every morning, 'accompanied, though not at that early hour, by several persons of distinction'. The regime began with a glass of water, after which the King would walk half an hour with his family, stopping to talk familiarly with passers by – 'everybody stopped or stood as they passed' – and visiting, no doubt,

from time to time the temple to the Goddess Cloacina strategi-
cally concealed a little down the hill from the spring. After the
second glass the party made its way home to breakfast over the
fields, the ladies in a carriage and his Majesty on foot. The time
between breakfast and four o'clock dinner was spent on horseback, the King plainly dressed because of the inclement
weather. It was on these rides that 'Farmer George' encountered
people of similar interests, and some of these meetings grew into
local legends. On one famous occasion he caught up with a
farmer driving a herd of sheep. The two men talked for a
quarter of an hour about the price of sheep and cattle.

> After satisfactorily answering all His Majesty's enquiries, the
> farmer asked the gentleman (as he thought) if he had seen
> the King; and, being answered in the affirmative, the farmer
> said, 'our neighbour says he's a good sort of man, but dresses
> very plain'. 'Aye', said His Majesty, 'as plain as you see me
> now', and rode on.

Indeed, 'nothing pleased the inhabitants so much as the
unguarded manner in which his Majesty lived, conversed, and
moved about among his faithful, his devoted subjects – like a
father in the midst of his children', though it is possible that the
plain dressing of the royal ladies disappointed the crowds that
flocked to the walks to see them. Only their straw bonnets were
worthy of comment, the Queen's and the Princess Royal's
elegantly trimmed with light green and white ribbons, Princess
Augusta's and Elizabeth's with light blue ones. The town was
overflowing. About thirty lodging-houses miraculously appeared
to fill the deficiency complained of for so many years and
visitors had to seek accommodation as far away as Tewkesbury.
Here and in Cheltenham landladies who had been satisfied
with three guineas the previous season were asking and re-
ceiving as much as twenty-five a week. While shops in the rest
of the country were busy advertising their 'Cheltenhamized'
products, the shops of Cheltenham itself were eager to put the
royal arms on their façades. The first citizen to cash in on this
form of publicity was John Boles Watson, who called after
breakfast on the King's first day at the Wells with a petition
that his theatre might be allowed to entertain the royal party.

'Leave was readily granted, with this further indulgence, that he might consider himself as immediately under the Royal protection.' Not a moment was wasted and the next day the bills bore the royal arms and the announcement of the week's programmes under the heading 'Theatre Royal'. 'About the same time a little fruit shop, that had the honour of vending some fruit to his Majesty, displayed a painted board inscribed, "Long Live the King!" with the name X X X Fruiterer to His Majesty.'

The principal attraction at the theatre was the Irish Dorothy Jordan, a Drury Lane comedienne celebrated for her Lady Teazle, her Rosalind and other 'breeches parts'. Little can George III have suspected as he applauded her performances that two years later she would begin a twenty-year liaison with his second son, the Duke of Clarence, that was to provide him with ten illegitimate grandchildren. Fanny Burney made three visits to the tiny theatre, but though she admired the leading lady the plays were too coarse for her taste.

> Mrs Jordan played *The Country Girl*, most admirably; but the play is so disagreeable in its whole plot and tendency, that all the merit of her performance was insufficient to ward off disgust. . . . [20 July]

> In the afternoon I went again to the play. . . . It was *Sir Harry Wildair* and Mrs Jordan performed it extremely well, but very little to my satisfaction. It is a very disagreeable play, and wholly abounding in all that can do violence to innocence and morality. . . . [30 July]

Like Fauconberg Hall, the theatre was hardly large enough to hold the royal party, and while they managed well enough in the early weeks it was stretched to overflowing on 1 August, when the Duke of York and his retinue arrived and expressed a wish for an evening at the play. Hasty orders were sent to prepare the royal box, but several of the gentlemen had to stand. Miss Burney and Miss Planta were accommodated in Mr de la Bere's own box near the stage, where they witnessed Mrs Jordan as Hippolyta in *She Would and She Would Not* and Roxalana in *The Sultan*. 'The delight of the people that their King and Queen should visit this country theatre was the most disinterested I ever witnessed; for though they had not even a glance of their Royal countenances, they shouted, huzzaed, and clapped for many minutes.'

The Duke's visit caused complications. Almost as soon as the King had arrived men had begun work in the grounds of Fauconberg Hall putting up a temporary wooden house for his son's reception. 'The task had employed 20 or 30 men almost since our arrival, and so laborious, slow, and all but impracticable it had proved that it was barely accomplished before it was wanted.'

The little household was not without its troubles, though they did not seem to affect the amiable King, so soon to be given up as a hopeless invalid and madman. Fanny diverted herself by fancying a romance with Mr Fairly, a dim widower unworthy of her lively mind, who came to drink tea in the little bit of passage outside her room which was the only place the ladies-in-waiting could find to hold sociable meetings. Poor Mr Fairly developed a fit of the gout and a swollen face and attributed them to the water-drinking. The King viewed his gentleman's transformation with unsympathetic satisfaction, remarking that the waters were 'admirable friends to the constitution, by bringing out disorders of the habit'.

The whole party removed for three days to take part in the Three Choirs Festival at Worcester. These concerts, in aid of the clergy orphans of Gloucestershire, Worcestershire and Herefordshire, had been taking place yearly since 1724 in each of the cathedrals alternately. The programme was principally of music by Handel. The performances were 'more numerously attended than ever before' and the orphans benefited to the tune of £500. In Worcester Fanny caught influenza and Miss Planta was the next victim, but the hard-pressed ladies, having nobody to stand in for them, were unable to take to their beds except for the occasional half-hour, and 'the Cheltenham episode', as Fanny called it, ended with both of them in low spirits.

On 16 August the royal party took their departure, and many other notabilities who had crowded Cheltenham to be with them – the Earls Oxford, Bathurst, Courtown and Harrington;

the Lords Rivers, Apsley, Maitland, Hamilton and Falkland; 'and all the fashion that Gloucester, Worcester and the County could send' – watched them go and then departed themselves. 'All Cheltenham was drawn out into the High Street, the gentles on one side and the commons on the other, and a band playing "God Save the King".' The music was supplied from 'Lord Harrington's Regiment, which had been sent to play every evening in the walks' and the "gentles" paraded in silent respect in front of Byrch's Coffee House. The royal party walked slowly between their subjects, high and lowly, bowing graciously to one side and the other.'

CHAPTER SEVEN

By the Waters of Cheltenham

KING GEORGE was kindly concerned about the supply of the health-giving water and it was not in any spirit of Sabbatarianism – a spirit not to descend on Cheltenham for another forty years – that he suggested banning its drinking on Sundays. It was a precaution to conserve its supply. There was evident anxiety about this, for a visiting doctor urged the inhabitants 'seeing that they have all the waters to themselves for seven months of the year . . . they should be a little more sparing of their draughts during the season'. George caused a new well to be bored in Lord Fauconberg's grounds. It was known as the King's Well, but was not destined to be one of the important springs of the future.

New springs were desperately needed, for the publicity of the royal visit stimulated invalids to flock to the town, but various circumstances – the French Revolution, the protracted wars with Napoleon, the bad roads and difficulty of transporting building-materials – slowed the growth of the Spa for another twenty years. Between George's visit and the end of the wars a frantic search went on for more and better water to assuage a thirst so fashionable at the turn of the century. Dr Jameson made over forty borings on the slope south of the present Queen's Hotel. Henry Thompson, a London merchant who bought the rolling pasture south and east of Skillicorne's well, later to be covered by the squares and crescents of the Montpellier and Lansdown districts, made double that number. New finds were made at Cambray when two springs of chalybeate water (strongly impregnated with iron) were located near Barrett's Mill.

Dr Jameson's first well was named Sherborne in compliment to the Dutton family, who continued Lords of the Manor and had recently been ennobled. It was in the vicinity of the present Suffolk Square, so called because the Earl of Suffolk built himself a mansion near the old Gallipot Farm. Here, in Jameson's rustic pump-room, three hogsheads of water (about 156 gallons) were consumed every day in the season until Thompson's rival borings further down towards the Chelt caused it to dry up, and the doctor had to explore elsewhere.

Thompson built his own house in a setting of lanes and pasture between Sherborne Well and the Serpentine Walks below the old spa. In this handsome stone building with its Doric colonnade he began his first pump-room. He later built himself another house, still standing, a little back from the Bath Road, christened Hygeia after the goddess of health, the presiding deity of the town, but renamed Vittoria House to celebrate Wellington's victory. In 1809 his first Montpellier Wells was opened, a long room of the *cottage ornée* type, with a verandah supported on wooden pillars, and a tree-lined approach in imitation of Skillicorne's well. The increasing number of visitors (3000 in 1801, but over 8000 in 1811) enabled him to replace this eight years later 'at almost incalculable expense' with the handsome pump-room that now survives as Lloyd's Bank, described in 1826 in Griffith's *History of Cheltenham*:

> It forms, in warm and cold weather, an equally agreeable and pleasant reception room; well ventilated throughout in summer, while it is protected from the intense heat of the solar rays to which it is exposed by its southern aspect; and rendered proof against the inclemency of the season, by the constant practice of heating by steam in winter.

At first the pump room was a simple oblong surrounded by a stone-pillared verandah, a lion couchant crowning its façade, but eight years later the owner's son, Pearson Thompson, called in Papworth, an architect celebrated for work in the Crimea and Egypt, to add the handsome Rotunda, 'a circular room, fifty-one feet in height, and fifty in diameter', supported by sixteen Corinthian pilasters and surmounted by the central dome which crowns the building. This room may still be visited in banking hours, its elegance not entirely obscured by the circle of counters. Two little coloured prints in the entrance remind the customer of the use for which this hall of commerce was originally intended, when 'from the seventh hour of the morning until nearly the tenth, the animation and gaiety continue unabated . . . whilst the soothing sound of music heightens the charm . . . revives the invalid's hope – and softens his affliction'.

Though the Montpellier Rotunda still stands, looking across the wide stretch of green that was once Henry Thompson's Rides and Walks, and beyond it stretch the beautiful squares and crescents that his son made into the Lansdown estate, the most important of the wells, from the point of view of Cheltenham's development, has been obliterated. This was the New Sherborne Spa, built lower down the hill to replace Dr Jameson's dried-up well. Before this pump-room was erected certain openings out of the High Street were beginning to grow into thoroughfares, and, before the nineteenth century, St George's Place appeared, a reasonably good carriage-road to Fauconberg Hall, running parallel to the Well Walk on the west. East of the walk a lane near the Market Hall was being transformed into the Colonnade, for which Lord Fauconberg laid the foundation stone in 1791. The uniting of this with the approach to the New Sherborne Spa was to determine the shape of the future town, for it became the Promenade and its development doomed Captain Skillicorne's attractive avenue to eventual obliteration. Where the new walk was laid out, Griffith described –

> a swampy and scarcely passable lane, leading from the High Street to the Chelt, over which the passenger could only cross 'upon the unsteadfast footing' of a plank; and when this feat was accomplished, an uncultured marsh on the other side, not only offended the sight, but from its often stagnant waters issued no wholesome exhalations.

But by 1826 the visitor could stand in the High Street and look towards

> a charming country prospect, of well diversified scenery, while his attention is attracted by, and then fixed upon, the

elegant structure situated on an easy eminence, which apparently terminates the well regulated carriage drive and wooded walks, upwards of a quarter of a mile in extent. Midway from the Colonnade the stream rolls its babbling tide through culverts, surmounted by lightly handsome iron railings on each side, which heighten the beauty of the spot, and, as barriers, protect the playful careless feet of infancy and youth from the water that flows beneath. On either side of the carriage road, trees and plants, the graceful mountain ash, the leafy sycamore, the birch, the beech, pine and larch, witch elms, and flowery shrubs, lend to the scene the charms of their varying foliage.

Where the Queen's Hotel now stands, the new Sherborne Pump Room, later the Imperial Spa, put up in 1818 by Samuel Harward and Thomas Henney, must have been Cheltenham's most charming building. Modelled on the Athenian Temple of Ilissus, it had a portico supported on six Ionic pillars and crowned with a dome 'on which stands a colossal statue of Hygiea'. This inevitable lady was described by an author less reverent than most as

> a bouncer, my lud!
> And as plump, ay, as any princess of the blood,
> Carved in stone, but a good imitation of wood.

The water flowed through 'cocks of pure crystal, expressly constructed for the purpose'; there was the usual 'band of musick' and a fruit and flower garden for the refreshment of subscribers.

In the Cambray district an octagon pump-room was put over the chalybeate well and another, of the same shape, built over a spring found at Alstone, but doomed to failure. Faced with this competition the owners of the original spa deepened their well in the hope of increasing the supply of water. In 1816 the Old Well suffered the loss of Hannah Forty, who died aged seventy-two, having been its pumper for over fifty years. So popular was she that Miller's pump-room was spoken of as 'Mrs Forty's Well' and she earned a memorial tablet in the church.

In the first year of the century communications with the outside world had been improved to the extent that a post office was opened in the shop of Mr Smith, a High Street grocer. Previous posts had been entrusted to one Sally Saunders, who wore a scarlet uniform cloak and carried letters in a basket, sometimes detaining them for 'five or six days after they had arrived, saying "she had something else to do than take a single letter to the bottom of the High Street" '. But even she had been an improvement on Nancy Wells, the bellwoman, toll collector, night watchman and special constable. Before Sally, she had been responsible for deliveries, effecting them 'at least within a fortnight after they had left the place from which they were sent'. From the grocer the post office was transferred to the ironmonger, but the arrangements continued 'extremely precarious' until after the Napoleonic wars.

The seasonal visitors came flocking in despite the insufficiency of transport, the condition of the roads and the continued shortage and expense of lodgings. It is difficult to imagine anything more charming that the appearance of the growing town during the years when it was visited by the Duke of Wellington. He came four times – in 1805 as a relatively unknown officer, sallow-faced and in poor health on his return from India; as a hero still trailing the glory of Waterloo in 1816; again in 1823, and, for the last time, in 1828, the year be became Prime Minister. The occasional visitor notices changes more than the resident, and Wellington, who first saw the town when 'the only conspicuous objects were . . . Fauconberg House and a double range of buildings in the High Street above the Plough . . . the only habitations considered fit for the reception of wealth and title', must have looked, on his last visit, on a considerable quantity of sparkling new Regency terraces and houses, their slim pillars, fantastic domes and delicate lace of wrought iron charmingly set off among the trees on the gentle slope on either side of the river.

Royal Crescent had already been started by the time of the Duke's first visit, a simple curve of eighteen houses on the west of Church Meadow facing Well Walk, with the first chain of Cheltenham's canopied iron balconies strung across its front, big sunny rooms and views to the Cotswolds. The 120 oil lamps burnt at night along the High Street and, on ball nights, a row of lights in the trees of the avenue. Arthur Wellesley, as he then was, came late in the season and remained, profiting from the cure, for a few weeks in September and early October. The visit fitted in between two moments of history – his one and only encounter with Lord Nelson, which had taken place on 12 September in an anteroom in the Colonial Office, and the Admiral's death at Trafalgar on the twenty-first of the next month. It was a time of perplexity for the thirty-six-year-old soldier. India had left him none too well; he was concerned about his brother's political career and about his own future in politics or war. He had come fresh from the society of the London courtesan Harriette Wilson to the mercies of the busy-body, Olivia Sparrow, who had determined to make him renew his proposal to Lord Longford's daughter, Kitty Paken-ham. Popular rumour, as well as Mrs Sparrow, told him Kitty had been pining, keeping faithful to him in Ireland since he had proposed to her in 1794, and said to be changed past recogni-tion. Letters were written. Wellesley renewed his proposal of eleven years before; Kitty replied in a guarded manner that he should see her again before committing himself to her for life. Whatever had happened to effect the alteration in the one-time rosy-cheeked girl, and there were rumours of smallpox (untrue) and of an abortive romance with a son of the Earl of Enni-skillen, Wellesley considered himself engaged. Only death in Hanover, if he should suddenly be called to fight there, could free him from the obligation he had entered into at the age of twenty-five. But there was diversion to be found in Cheltenham, whatever his private perplexities. His cousin, 'Mrs Wellesley-Pole, had given him an introduction to a French emigré countess and her friend Mrs Upton; and there was a moment of drama worthy of his favourite amateur theatricals. The countess's garter fell off as they left the Pump Room, Arthur picked it up with the appropriate words *"Honi soit qui mal y pense"*, and Mrs Upton whispered sardonically in the countess's ear, "Lucky it was a new one!" '

The next year saw the passing of the second Paving Act, which declared the streets, both new and old, to be 'incom-modious, unsafe for passengers and not sufficiently lighted'. The seventy-two Commissioners appointed to carry out the Act's provisions included Robert, son of Thomas Hughes of the Assembly Rooms; the Reverend Richard Nash Skillicorne, heir to the Captain's property; the Earl of Suffolk; Thomas Baghott de la Bere; John Boles Watson of the Theatre Royal; and Colonel John Riddell, a notable eccentric and medical quack who managed to 'remain inactive in the military sense for the whole of the Napoleonic wars', but, after they had ended, entertained their hero in his house in Cambray, which was promptly rechristened Wellington Mansion. Other names on the list were to become famous in the future – Joseph Pitt, who was to found Pittville, and Dr Edward Jenner, destined for celebrity far beyond Gloucestershire as the discoverer of vaccination.

Jenner had been born in Berkeley village and was recommended to Cheltenham water at the age of forty-six, when his health had been broken by an attack of cholera. He made influential friends in the town, a place now full of famous doctors attending on illustrious invalids taking the water cure made fashionable by King George. His historic experiment with cowpox had been made at Berkeley and he was in Cheltenham at the time of the publication of his *Inquiry* into the effect of the treatment. 'As a matter of fact, Cheltenham was the only place in the length and breadth of the kingdom where Jenner was completely accepted and encouraged in his work.' Listed as a resident physician in 1800, he lived first at Alpha House, still standing in St George's Road, and then bought No. 8 St George's Place from Colonel Riddell. This narrow road was to become the Harley Street of Cheltenham, with Dr Newell, Physician Extraordinary to George IV, at No. 5 and at least four other eminent medical men. No. 8 has recently been pulled down. The celebrated preacher, Rowland Hill, a friend of Jenner's and an advocate of vaccination, came frequently to take services at the Chapel for Dissenters on the opposite side of the road – now falling down and hidden from view, with its graveyard, behind the houses. Hill was always ready to operate on volunteers after his sermons. 'The learned parson probably vaccinated more people than any other non-medical person.'

The town was putting out feelers down every country lane

that meandered into the High Street, transforming them into elegant terraces for visitors, from Cambray to the Colonnade, and into rows of humble dwellings for artisans west of the church. Further building of terraces, crescents and detached villas began to surround the Montpellier Rotunda above Sherborne Spa. The charm of these houses lay in the variety of delicate ironwork, in balconies, porches and railings, their intricate patterns making shadows against the honey-coloured Cotswold stone or pale painted stucco, diverting attention from the plain outlines and gimcrack nature of many Regency buildings. Like the Nash terraces in London's Regent's Park, the houses were run up in a hurry to meet a fashionable need. All interest was concentrated on magnificent frontages, and rows of solid-looking buildings had backs to them as featureless as tenements. Nevertheless the character of a village contrived to remain despite the Commissioners' efforts to banish Mops and Fairs from the town centre. Henrietta Street specialized in pigs; Albion Street in the sale of horses. 'It forms a curious and amusing sight to behold the mixture of London elegance with Gloucestershire fashion; to view the street with its booths . . . decorated with ribands and trinkets, and the crowding to-gether of rustic lads and Bond Street beaux – of rural lasses and Westminster belles.'

The war, extending over four continents, had little effect upon the town, apart from slowing its expansion. A citizen unfortunate enough to have his name drawn in the half-hearted Vestry ballot for the Militia was generally able to pay for a substitute. The Press Gang rarely penetrated so far inland. A local Volunteer Cavalry Force, and an Infantry one under Captain Hicks, were raised, the latter swearing to jump to and serve their King and Country on demand 'at any place within eight miles of Cheltenham'. A play, *The Marriage Promise*, was given to collect money for their uniforms; Watson devoted a night's takings at his theatre to providing comforts for the men in Flanders. French prisoners were allowed to mingle freely in the town's social life if they gave an undertaking that they would not go out further than three miles. This happy situation ended when the popular General Lefèvre upset his Cheltenham friends

by breaking parole. With his wife disguised as a boy he made
his way to London, and thence to France to rejoin Napoleon's
army.

Simon Moreau died in 1810 and was commemorated by a
flat stone in the aisle of the church. His successor, James King,
managed to combine the function of M.C. at Bath (he is
mentioned in *Northanger Abbey*) and at Cheltenham, for the
seasons – winter in Bath and summer at Cheltenham – did not
overlap. His reign lasted six years and on his death Alexander
Fotheringham was appointed. This was in the year of Wellington's second visit, when the town's popularity had reached its
height, earning it the title 'the merriest sick-resort on earth'.
Visitors in the ten intervening years had included members of
the royal family – the Regent, and his cousin, the Duke of
Gloucester, who continued to come yearly from 1807. Dorothy
Jordan, the actress who had delighted George III in the local
theatre, was practically one of them. She had returned to act a
number of times since then, when she was not occupied in
presenting the king with illegitimate grandchildren. It was in
1811, while acting for John Boles Watson, that she received the
shattering news that the Duke of Clarence felt it necessary to
end their twenty years of happy union. Exiled French royalty
came – Marie-Antoinette's glum daughter, the Duchesse
d'Angoulême and her husband; her uncle and father-in-law
Louis XVIII, unavailingly recommended by George III to try
the waters for his gout; his brother the Comte d'Artois, later
Charles X. A third future occupant of the French throne was
Louis-Philippe, Duc d'Orléans, who came in 1816 and stayed
three months. The local press published Cheltenham's weekly
score in dukes and duchesses, marquises and marchionesses,
bishops and earls, counts, lords and ladies, besides Hons and
Barts and foreigners of title.

> Men of every class and order,
> All the genera and species,
> Dukes with Aides-de-Camp in leashes,
> Marquises in tandem traces,
> Lords in couples, counts in pairs,
> Coveys of their spendthrift heirs.

Hosts of soldiers, shoals of seamen,
Droves of squires and herds of farmers,
Swarms of dandies, flocks of charmers,
Troops of half-pay light dragoons,
Stores of cockneys, heaps of spoons;
Cabinets of politicians,
Ins and outs of whole divisions;
Heaps of lawyers, surgeons, proctors,
Lots of nurses, dentists, doctors,
Hovering round as ravens do.

Cheltenham is thus observed to be
All mankind's epitome,
A sort of general congregation
Culled from every tribe and nation –
English, Irish, Welsh and Scottish,
French, Dutch, Flemish, Hottentottish,
Swiss, Italian, Spanish, German,
Russ with collar lined with ermine,
Jolly Danskers, Swedes, Norwegians,
Esquimaux from Polar Regions,
Austere Barons with their poodles,
Tartars, Turks and Yankee Doodles.

The distinguished visitors spent their evenings in the tiny
theatre, watching the now established Sarah Siddons, Charles
Kemble, Dorothy Jordan, Harriot Mellon and Grimaldi. There
was equal enjoyment of the amateur performances by Colonel
Berkeley and his brothers, the spectacle of English nobility on
the stage being, if possible, more diverting than that of the
professional players. Berkeley was a frequent host to Lord
Byron at the Castle. While in town Byron stayed at Georgiana
Cottage, on the corner of Bath Street in Cambray, with 'a very
pleasant set . . . the Jerseys, Melbournes, Cowpers and
Hollands'. He felt desolate when they left and wrote to Lord
Holland, sending respects to his Lady – 'Her departure, with
that of my other friends, was a sad event to me, now reduced
to a most cynical solicitude. "By the waters of Cheltenham I sat
down and *drank*, when I remembered thee, oh Georgiana
Cottage!" . . . I am dumb and dreary as the Israelites. The
waters have disordered me to my heart's content!'

In the spring of 1816 Jane Austen defected from her beloved

Bath for three weeks in Cheltenham and drank at the same pump (but which of the many then in use is not known) as the Duchesse d'Orléans. Her sister Cassandra was there in September, finding 'much to be satisfied with . . . while the waters agree, everything else is trifling'. Jane fancied that the spa was 'much to be preferred in May' and thought people foolish to pay exorbitant rents for the sake of saying they had lodgings in the High Street – a remark which suggests this thoroughfare had been effectively cleaned since Captain Skillicorne's day.

Between Jane's and Cassandra's visits Arthur Wellesley, now Duke of Wellington, made his second one, his presence sending up prices which had been rising steadily ever since the King had honoured the town. Wellington had not been feeling well since the peace, shuttled to and fro between Paris and the Netherlands at the beck and call of kings and politicians and with frequent London banquets with the Regent. A cure had been prescribed him. Waterloo was a year behind, but his reception was as rapturous as if it had been the day before – the Regency passion for illuminations and transparencies running riot. Kitty Pakenham, now his Duchess and the mother of two sons, arrived on 5 July. He followed two days later, entering his Cambray lodging from the High Street through a triple wooden arch, painted to look like stone and adorned with his portrait and the names of his victories. Colonel Riddell poured out water from the medicinal well in his Cambray garden, chased down by copious draughts of 'old fine-flavoured East India Madeira'. Colonel Berkeley made the address of welcome, praising the victories and ending with 'our most fervent prayer, that the object which has procured us the honour of your Grace's visit, may be speedily crowned with the happiest results to yourself and the country'. Between public appearances and visits to Berkeley Castle the Duke drank at the old well and delighted his wife by finding plenty of time to spend with their sons. 'He for whom the whole world is so justly anxious is considerably better both in looks and spirits', she wrote,

> . . . I think I perceive an amendment every day. This happens to be the time of the holiday of our Boys, and I say with delight they are as fond of and as familiar with their noble

and beloved Father as if they had never been separated from him. They accompany him on his walks, chat with him, play with him. In short they are the chosen companions of each other.

The Duke found Cheltenham less animated than the local journals would have their readers believe and informed his adoring Lady Shelley after three days, 'I am already so well that I believe half the world take me for a malingerer. . . . I am obliged to live quietly here, there being nobody here excepting the Duchess and my boys and Lord Lynedock, who is come down to see me, and some few sick and wounded officers of the army.'

Wellington planted an oak tree in Colonel Riddell's garden to commemorate his visit, but his principal public duty was to open new assembly rooms at a glittering ball on 29 July. An austerely fronted building in the High Street, on the site now occupied by a branch of Lloyd's Bank, housed a magnificent ballroom, splendid with Corinthian pilasters and chandeliers, commodious card-rooms and an entrance hall 120 feet long. Thomas Hughes's former rooms, built only thirty years earlier, had been pulled down as inadequate in a somewhat ruthless manner. Not everyone could gain admission to the new Rooms and the guide books advised the visitor to obtain a 'letter of introduction from their friends, who may have previously resided here, or may be acquainted with the resident or visiting families of the town'. 'No clerk, hired or otherwise in this town or neighbourhood' was admitted, 'no person concerned in retail trade; no theatrical or other public performers by profession'. Those who did have the honour to be allowed inside had to be careful of their dress, for 'no gentleman in boots or half-boots' could be tolerated on ball nights 'except officers in the navy or army in uniform; and undress trowsers or coloured pantaloons cannot be permitted on any account'. High society had indeed altered the informality of Cheltenham since pre-royal-visit days, when no public place had been 'so free from restraints as this'.

Wellington evidently profited from his stay – the waters and the relative peace of his holiday – for Lady Arbuthnot wrote early in September to let Lady Shelley know that 'the sun', as his bevy of ladies called him, 'shines *bright*. He is really wonderfully improved by Cheltenham, and got a brown, healthy colour, and seems to have got his head and stomach quite right.'

CHAPTER EIGHT

The Devouring Wen

COLONEL WILLIAM FITZHARDINGE BERKELEY, who had spoken so eloquently at the reception for Wellington, was the principal moving spirit of Regency Cheltenham and its generous benefactor. Eldest son of the foolish Fifth Earl, he had been brought up to believe he would succeed his father; had called himself Lord Dursley (the proper title of the heir) and Earl of Berkeley after his father's death, until the trial of his legitimacy before the Lords made the family name and history an open scandal. The Fifth Earl and Mary Cole, daughter of a Gloucestershire butcher, produced Fitz, as he was known in the family, as the first of seven illegitimate children before their legal marriage in 1796. Mary Cole was then pregnant with her eighth child, Thomas Moreton, who was, the House decided in 1811, the rightful Sixth Earl. The father of Fitz and all the Berkeley progeny, legitimate and illegitimate, had not intended to marry at all, assuming that a butcher's daughter would be flattered to be made mistress of a nobleman. But Mary was not only beautiful and virtuous, she was a woman of character, intelligence and financial acumen – finding her lover's estates in a deplorable condition, she asked permission to take over their management and liquidated his debts in the course of a year. Tricked by the Earl, who could not get her to bed by other means, into a faked marriage in Berkeley church, she eventually persuaded him to make her his legal wife. She fought all her life, with some help from the Prince Regent, to legitimize her adored Fitz, whom she had brought up to believe he was his father's heir, by proving the validity of the first ceremony. With experience of society the butcher's daughter so developed her natural qualities that she became a favourite guest at the Regent's Brighton Pavilion. After her husband's death she even had the chance to make herself Queen, when she was proposed to by the Duke of Clarence, later William IV – an offer she declined in a tactfully worded letter to his brother.

The nickname 'Fitz', with its ready-made suggestion of the wrong side of the blanket, may seem an unfortunate choice for one who hoped to prove his legitimacy, but the name went back to an ancestor, Robert Fitzhardinge, a wealthy Bristol merchant who received Berkeley Castle from Henry II as a reward for help in the wars against Stephen. Young Fitzhardinge was intelligent and must have realized that the magnificent feast held at Berkeley to celebrate his coming of age might turn out a hollow pretence. When the Lords rejected his claim and he had to abandon the Earldom to his brother, he adopted the title Colonel Berkeley which he held in the Gloucestershire Yeomanry, while Thomas Moreton, under his mother's influence, refused to accept his inheritance and remained un-married so as not to pass it to his heirs. He allowed the Colonel to remain in possession of the castle.

Opinions differ sharply on the character of the man who might have been Earl. His interest in politics – he was a Whig, belonging to a party that was Liberal 'chiefly in so far as they desired that power should rest with the nobility rather than the Crown' – and his excellence as a speaker, should have destined him for Parliament, but to sit in the Commons would have been to admit he had no right to a seat in the Lords and to betray all his mother had fought for. He therefore wasted his talents, living principally in Gloucestershire, a life dedicated to sport – the Berkeley Hunt was famous throughout the country, the close of its season marked with a procession through Chelten-ham, bells pealing from the parish church; to theatricals, of a standard high enough to compare with professionals; and to the begetting of more illegitimate Berkeleys – at one time there were said to be thirty-three within ten miles of the castle, and maids could not be got to work there. He was popular with sportsmen; tolerated by farmers and landowners, for he paid up promptly for damage done by his hounds; a good companion; a linguist; an excellent host. But some, like Harriette Wilson, thought him ostentatious, and there is little doubt that his extraordinary childhood and his mother's extravagant devotion had spoilt a character that might have been remarkable.

Berkeley Castle did not scruple to shelter the theatrical performers denied entrance to the Assembly Rooms; the great Grimaldi was an occasional visitor and the Colonel lent his Cheltenham residence, German Cottage, for the entertainment of ladies of doubtful reputation. Society winked at such foibles of the nobility, for snobbery rather than prudery dictated taboos in Regency times and the Colonel added vastly to the town's prosperity. In 1819 he gave a thousand pounds to assist the Cheltenham Races, which began on Cleeve Hill, with subscriptions, besides, from Lord Sherborne and others. By 1823, the time of Wellington's third visit, they had moved to their present situation at Prestbury, where the course 'commanded the most extensive view of all the surrounding country', the turf being considered 'by judicious sportsmen, as equal, if not superior, to any in the kingdom'.

The principal roads, the responsibility of the Turnpike Commissioners, had been somewhat improved by the 1820s. Beyond the Upper Turnpike at the east end of the High Street, the London Road had been realigned through Dowdeswell to Andoversford. The new Bath Road ran south from Cambray through Shurdington and Painswick with a branch through Leckhampton. Beyond the Lower Turnpike an important new road had been made to Gloucester along the line of a horserailway by which, since 1809, trucks had been dragged to supply the town with coal and stone. The construction of this led to the decline of the old Gloucester Road through Prestbury and Swindon which crossed the Tewkesbury Road a mile beyond the Turnpike. The lower part of this runs, to this day, through an unspoilt stretch of country. These new roads, each of which required separate acts of Parliament, were kept in a sorry state of repair and were apt to become rivers in wet weather.

S. Y. Griffith's history of the Spa, published in 1826, had a

map showing its development at that time. This can be com-
pared with the plan made after the Inclosure Act of 1801, an
Act which had paved the way for expansion, abolishing the
system of open fields and permitting building on the Marsh, the
'Rotten Row of the place' where Byng had enjoyed riding. With
Griffith's map in hand the modern visitor can reconstruct a
picture of the town as it looked to the motley crowd that
flocked there during the Regency.

To the west of the churchyard, its lime avenues not yet
hemmed in with buildings, St George's Place ran south to
Bayshill. Continuing along the south side of the High Street
the visitor came next to the elegant curve of Royal Crescent and
then to the Colonnade, which 'although commenced so many
years ago, has never been completed, a circumstance at which
we should rejoice, since we now behold so very superior a range
of buildings in the Sherborne Promenade, delightfully dis-
playing the "rus in urbe" '. This terrace still stands, now uniformly painted green and occupied by the Municipal offices, but
for all its handsome front, its pediment and Ionic pilasters, its
undistinguished rear spoilt the charming outlook from Royal
Crescent. Near the new Assembly Rooms the smart area of
Cambray contained Bath Street, site of Byron's beloved
Georgiana Cottage, leading to the new Bath Road with its
medicinal baths, Thompson's Vittoria House, and, further
south, J. R. Scott's Thirlestaine House, a palatial mansion on
which this newcomer spent nearly £20,000, leaving it unfinished
at his death. This, the most substantial private house the town
was ever to see, was yet another version of the Temple of
Ilissus, with a portico supported on Ionic columns. It now
stands, with added wings, as part of Cheltenham College. Just
short of Scott's great house and west of the Bath Road, the
Montpellier Walks led to the Spa, the Earl of Suffolk's house
and 'some delightful edifices, which have invariably been
occupied by families of the first distinction'.

North along the High Street, above the churchyard, Henrietta
Street ran towards the Marsh, soon to be swallowed under
bricks and mortar. Opposite the Colonnade North Street led to
Albion Street and St Margaret's Terrace. Winchcombe Street

ran parallel and Grosvenor Place, leading to Gloucester and Sherborne Places. Beyond Cambray and the Bath Road a number of smaller streets branched towards the Cotswolds with a mixed collection of new villas and old thatched cottages. One familiar feature had vanished from the High Street – Richard Pate's ancient but comfortable almshouses which had been left in the care of Corpus Christi. Complaints had been made that the sixteenth-century building looked incongruous in the smartened High Street and that it had fallen into disrepair. The college, therefore, exchanged it with a banker, Thomas Smith, for a site less than a fifth its area. A solid plain house of Cotswold stone was built in Albion Street, which still stands and houses pensioners, but the old people lost their spacious garden and their chapel for a situation less open and pleasant. The exchange was contrary to the spirit of Pate's legacy, which should, in any event, have been used to keep the original building in good repair. Smith sold the site for £2000. It is now occupied by the extension to Woolworths. The High Street also exhibited a market hall, the fourth to be built in a century – an oriental–Gothic extravaganza opened in 1823 by Lord Sherborne. Through a triple arch surmounted by his family arms the shoppers found a double row of stalls for meat, poultry, fish and greengrocery, covered on one side, open to the weather on the other.

A quantity of churches and chapels, in every possible style for every possible persuasion, began to arise during the Regency. A small Benedictine chapel in Clarence Street catered for refugees from the Revolution and, later, for members of the French royal family in exile. Before 1810 the Abbé César had said mass for his flock in a room in the York Hotel. In 1816 a chapel was constructed in North Place for the Countess of Huntingdon's (Wesleyan) Connection in an odd mixture of the prevailing classical taste with future fashion in which Doric columns combined with Gothic windows. G. A. Underwood, who created this and the enchanting Sherborne Spa, went on to design Holy Trinity, the first Anglican building to supplement the ancient parish church, which was bursting at the seams, having had to install a succession of galleries to accommodate the overflow of visitors since the King's visit of 1788. The style of the new church, completed in 1823, was more completely Gothic, a style which did not suit the designer of Cheltenham's first little Grecian temple. His Masonic Hall, modelled on a Roman mausoleum, was better suited to his talents. Cheltenham possessed a quantity of wealthy Masons, including Robert Hughes, son of the owner of the Assembly Rooms, who built himself the attractive Rodney Lodge, which still stands in the road of that name. Another charming private house, Albion Villa in North Street, belonged to Theodore Gwinnett, clerk to the Commissioners. It is now the Liberal Club.

The Impropriation of the parish church had been bought in 1800 by Joseph Pitt, one of the seventy-two commissioners of the second Paving Act. Twelve years later he obtained the right to appoint its ministers by handing over the living of Bagendon, Gloucestershire, in his gift, to the Fellows of Jesus College in exchange for the advowson which they had held since the days of Sir Baptist Hicks. This put an end to the succession of Welsh names in the list of incumbents. Pitt's beginnings had been humble. Like Shakespeare he had come to the notice of those able to advance him while holding horses for a penny a time. A Cirencester attorney took a fancy to the 'sharp lad' and trained him to his own business. It was not long before he was making enough money to buy land, and by 1812 had 'a clear landed estate of £20,000 a year'. By his purchase of the Rectory, Pitt became owner of Cambray and Church Meadows and, by exchange of his right to receive tithes, possessor of 189 acres in the Marsh. By the time the Inclosure Act permitted owners to fence their fields, use them for their own purposes or sell them for building, he had made himself the greatest landowner in Cheltenham. It was on the Marsh that he began, early in the 1820s, to build his own town of Pittville, with its spacious terraces, broad tree-lined walks, its park and magnificent pump-room. In 1825, two years after Wellington's third visit, the foundation stone for this, the largest and most handsome of Cheltenham's Spas, was laid with full Masonic ritual and a service in the parish church. The banking crisis later in the same year, which ruined many prosperous merchants, held up the progress of the building, and when the Duke returned in 1828, the year he became Prime Minister, Pitt's Pump Room was not yet open to the public.

The development of Pitt's town was sourly observed by William Cobbett, who visited the 'devouring wen' on one of his *Rural Rides* in 1821, and, incensed on behalf of the poor by the Inclosure Act, which had, in fact, created little hardship in Cheltenham, disliked what he saw – 'a nasty, ill-looking place, half clown and half cockney. The town is all one street about a mile long; but then, at some distance from this street, there are rows of white tenements, with green balconies, like those inhabited by the tax-eaters round London.' The people who resorted to such places were stigmatized as 'East India plunderers, West India floggers, English tax-gorgers, together with gluttons, drunkards and debauchees of all descriptions, female as well as male, [who] resort, at the suggestion of silently laughing quacks, in the hope of getting rid of the bodily consequences of their manifold sins and iniquities'. A year after Pitt laid the foundation stone of the Pump Room Cobbett was back and delighted to learn from a coal-carter that the building work north of the Chelt was 'nearly at a stand'.

We rode up the main street of the town for some distance, and then turned off to the left which soon brought us to the 'desolation of abomination'. I have seldom seen anything with more heartfelt satisfaction. 'Oh!' I said to myself, 'the accursed *thing* has certainly got a *blow*, then, in every part of its corrupting carcass!' The whole town (and it was now ten o'clock) looked delightfully dull. I did not see more than four or five carriages, and, perhaps, twenty people on horseback; and these seemed by their hook-noses and round eyes, and by the long sooty necks of the women, to be, for the greater part, *Jews and Jewesses*. The place really seems to be sinking very fast; and I have been told, and believe the fact, that houses, in Cheltenham, will now sell for only just one-third as much as the same would have sold for only in last October. It is curious to see the names which the vermin owners have put upon the houses here. . . . There is '*Liverpool Cottage*', '*Canning Cottage*', '*Peel Cottage*'; and the good of it is, that the ridiculous beasts have put this word *cottage* upon scores of houses, and some very mean and shabby houses, standing along, and making part of an unbroken street! What a figure this place will cut in another year or two!

The vindictive Cobbett would have been annoyed to see the partial revival in Cheltenham's fortunes during the next five years, but his prophecy was not altogether inaccurate. The town was about to undergo transformation, though the change was from one sort of popularity to another. The fashion for medicinal spas had passed its peak and was going into rapid decline, and Pitt had planned and built his splendid resort, which he intended to be separate from and a rival to Cheltenham, just too late.

Cobbett would have detested Cheltenham's social leader had he known him, for Colonel Berkeley's way of life represented all this champion of the underdog most disapproved. He could have found some satisfaction, had he been aware of it, at the appointment, two years before his second visit, of a curate-in-charge at the parish church who was destined to become the uncrowned king of a reformed Cheltenham and the avowed antagonist of all that made the life of the Regency, and of the Colonel in particular, colourful and gay. Pitt had sold the advowson of St Mary's to an Evangelical body known as the Simeon Trust and it was under the new regime that the Reverend Francis Close had been appointed. Though Cobbett would not have cared personally for a clergyman who managed to make himself *persona grata* in the richest houses, particularly with the women, he could not have failed to rejoice in the sombre shadow this opponent of all gaiety and progress, of races, theatres and railways, was to cast on the frivolous life of the 'devouring wen'.

On either side of Cobbett's last visit the Duke of Wellington made two more, to take the baths as well as drink the waters which had previously restored his health. This time he did not stay at Colonel Riddell's 'Wellington Mansion', scene of his last rapturous welcome, but rented another villa in Cambray which was subsequently renamed Wellington House, making the whole town, with its Vittoria House and Hotel and the new Wellington Square in Pittville, into something of a personal monument.

In 1828, now Prime Minister, he returned on 15 August, 'white and overworked', for a fortnight's relaxation. Whatever the journals might say of the place, Wellington had never found Cheltenham anything but modestly rural, though the town's excitement, by the accounts in the local press, almost equalled that of 1816. This time he stayed at The Priory, a little out of town on the London Road, the residence of the new M.C., Captain Marshall, who had served him in the Peninsula. He was up early each morning to drink two glasses at the Old Well, with a twenty-minute walk in the elm avenue between. He mingled half an hour with the crowd at Montpellier Spa to listen to the band that played from eight o'clock until ten. On the way to breakfast he would drop into Mr Abraham's, the optician at the corner of the Pump Room, tap his barometer and exchange pleasantries about the weather, or wander into Mawe's Museum, which specialized in minerals and replicas of famous vases and models of the Leaning Tower, Cleopatra's Needle and other world-renowned objects. After breakfast he attended to the vast correspondence inseparable from his new office; went riding for an hour or two in the country, and returned for the prescribed hour of soaking. So as not to lose valuable time he entered the water with a sheaf of journals. 'Always the White Knight, he had a frame put across the bath to support his paper, thus solving a problem that has often baffled meaner intellects'. His evenings were quiet and he seldom went out after dinner, except to see Madame Vestris in *The Rencountre* at Watson's Theatre; for an hour to the Promenade Ball at the Montpellier Rotunda on the twenty-first; and to another ball given in his honour in the Assembly Rooms he had opened. He was acclaimed by 6000 people, a band playing 'See the Conquering Hero', and a transparency of Britannia holding his likeness on a medal in her hand. Princes Schwarzenburg and Esterhazy were of the company; with the Dukes of Buckingham, Beaufort and Manchester, and the Earls of Derby, Bathurst and Beauchamp. Cobbett had not been entirely right in his predictions. The noble rats had not yet deserted the sinking ship.

All this time, on the hill to the east of the Evesham Road, the

Pittville Pump Room was slowly being built, half-way between the High Street and the race course. Pittville Street, widened under the 1821 Act of Parliament from the original Portland Passage, led to it through large oblong gardens, planted with a variety of trees, many of which – evergreen oaks, sycamores and beeches, both the green and copper varieties – still stand, their branches sweeping the lawns like graceful crinolines. To either side stretched terraces of tall houses, the 'white tenements' of Cobbett's scorn with their 'green balconies', varied with an occasional free-standing mansion. To the west stood two squares, named for Wellington and the Duke of Clarence, soon to be William IV, their gardens planted with silver birch, golden-leaved in autumn against the dark olive of further evergreen oaks; to the east curved a graceful crescent. The main thoroughfare led to a less formal garden with an artificial lake, climbing to the orange Cotswold stone temple, the most elaborate and tallest of Cheltenham's pump-rooms, a two-storied building surmounted by a dome and surrounded by a colonnade of fluted columns with elaborately carved capitals. Hygeia, inevitably, dominated the centre, with figures of Hippocrates and Aesculapius over the wings. The upper floor commanded a fine view of the town, with the Cotswolds providing a frame at the back. Inside was the oblong hall or ballroom, with the spa, containing the marble drinking-fountain, opening out of its northern side. The great dome soared over the centre of the hall, seen through the open well of the first-floor gallery which provided a circular promenade for spectators to look down on the dancing. The architect was the Cheltenham resident, John Forbes, though some critics believe that Papworth, designer of the Montpellier Rotunda, may have had a hand in the work.

But the splendid project was doomed to failure and Pitt to the loss of much money. 'The expense of the materials, the remuneration of the architect, and the various artists and artisans, with the wages of the labourers employed, may fairly be estimated at little short of £90,000.' On 20 July 1830 the Pump Room was opened at a great public breakfast with Marshall, the M.C., presiding. The ceremony had had to be

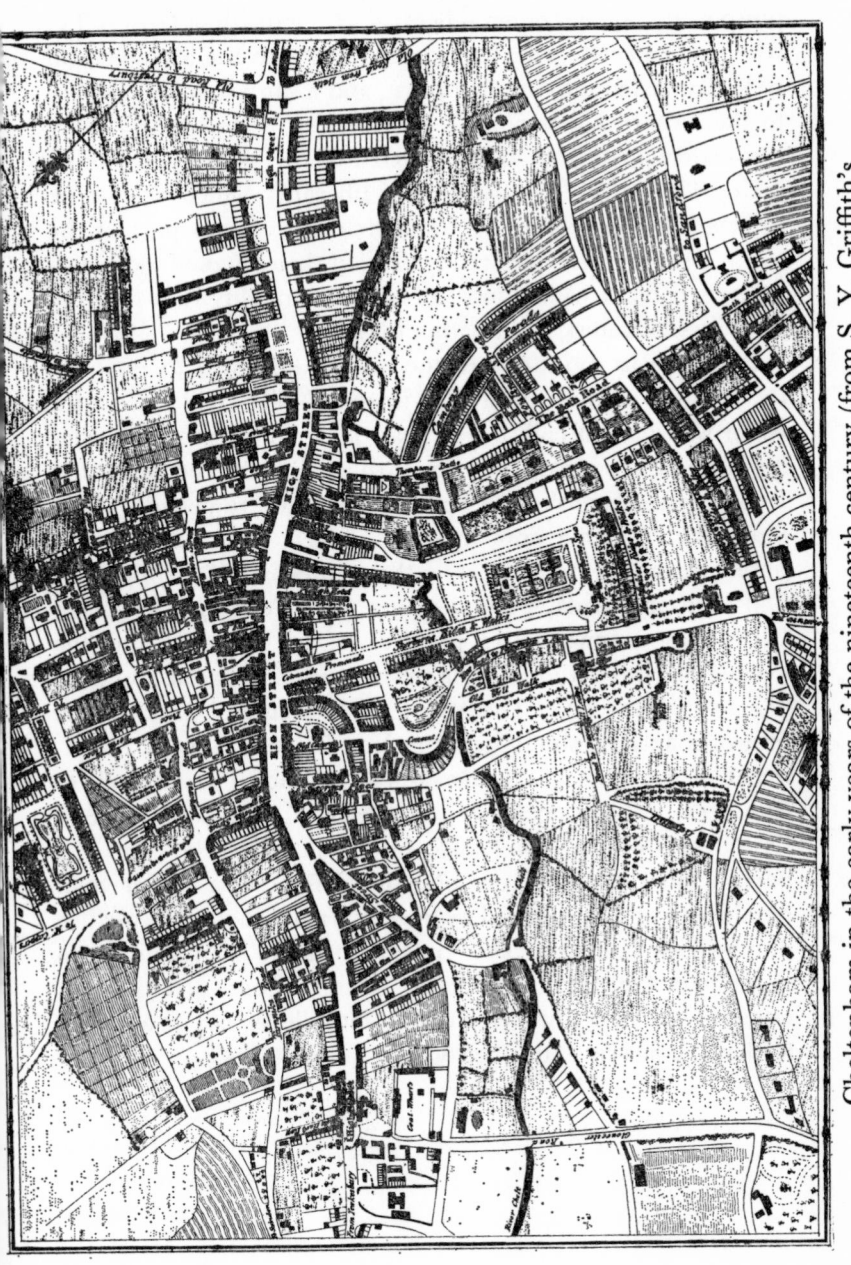

Cheltenham in the early years of the nineteenth century (from S. Y. Griffith's *New Historical Description of Cheltenham*, 1826)

postponed – an evil omen – because of the death of George IV, who, as Prince Regent, had given a name to the architectural style that lasted into his own reign, and a spirit and atmosphere to the days of Cheltenham's greatest glory. During the delay the waters had been offered free to 'any person by simply asking for them – an instance of liberality which cannot be sufficiently appreciated by those residents of that part of the town, and several have already availed themselves of the indulgence' – a boast which does not suggest a mighty rush to drink the Pittville waters, even without charge.

Pittville was too far from the town, and failed to establish the separate identity its creator intended. The public thirst for water was near its end. Seven years later Underwood's charming Imperial Spa, opened in 1818 as the Sherborne Pump Room, was demolished to be rebuilt in the Promenade where the A.B.C. Cinema now stands. The next year, 1838, saw a public breakfast to celebrate the centenary of Skillicorne's Old Well and Walk, when a young tree, 'the Royal Victorian Oak', was ceremoniously planted in the orchard, and the avenue lit with a thousand lamps in arches of green and gold like a cathedral nave. The music, processions and dancing, the fireworks and the simulated eruption of Vesuvius, were reminiscent of the days of the Royal visit; a medal was struck to commemorate the occasion and presented to the new young Queen at Buckingham Palace by Colonel Berkeley. But the party seemed to mark the obsequies of the Spa rather than heralding any new reign of prosperity. In another ten years this pump-room had also been pulled down, to be rebuilt as a music-hall. Only the Montpellier Rotunda remained popular, but, with the new white elephant at Pittville, chiefly as a setting for balls, concerts and other occasional festivities.

CHAPTER NINE

Close Quarters

THE water-drinking fashion was dying its slow death; the visitors rising later, abandoning their early morning stroll between the glasses to spend more time at 'cards, cards, cards, nothing but cards "from rosy morn to dewy eve" '. The ageing soldiers who flocked to the Spa for the sake of their livers passed the evening of their lives endlessly refighting Boney's wars or reliving their Indian exploits in conversation at the New Club in the Assembly Rooms before they faded away, to be commemorated, if they lasted till after 1840, in the marvellously elaborate mural tablets of the smart new Christ Church, a really successful essay in the Victorian Gothic. Those who paraded the streets in the mild damp weather struck observers as 'resolute idlers' with a 'lounging, indolent, do-nothing air'. Among those gaudily dressed 'fashionable butterflies' an increasing number of black 'Evangelical beetles' were observed following in the wake of the Reverend Francis Close.

The appearance of the little market town was altered for ever.

Yes, all are gone that mark'd the rural scene!
  No more thy groves and orchards meet the eye,
And where thy humble dwellings once had been,
  Stand now thy sculptured buildings tow'ring high,
And gilded spires that sweep the azure sky,
  And sweeping terraces and grand parades,
And circling crescents! Oh, what place can vie
  With thy fair avenues and cooling shades,
Or boast such beauteous forms as throng thy promenades!

Griffith's guide-book pointed out facts about Cheltenham that remain as true for the present town as they were for the one of 1826.

However surrounding buildings may yet increase . . . the town must ever hold within its bosom a grateful variety of umbrageous walks, and an enchanting display of rural scenery. Cupidity has shown itself wise by sacrificing to liberality! and the bold speculation, which, disdaining the usual narrow limits of a town house site, at a paltry price *per foot*, laid out its terraces, its pleasure grounds, its attached inclosures, its plantations, walks and approaches – worthy the environs of a palace . . . and secured a freedom and magnificence of appearance that the ancient and venerable city can never possess, and that few modern ones will ever rival.

Such open spaces included the lawns of Pittville, climbing to the Pump Room gardens, where, in 1836, a Grand Fête was held – 'a dream of enchantment; the illuminations were brilliant and dazzling; the lake girdled with a zone of light'. The Park, another green oasis, was developed by Thomas Billings, a hundred acres falling in a tear-drop shape to the south of Suffolk Square and girdled with large houses in their gardens. Originally intended for a zoo, it was converted, after financial failure, into a pleasure ground with cricket fields, archery butts and flower-lined walks.

But the Pittville fireworks, followed two years later by the centenary of the Old Well, were the swan song of Regency extravagance. Instead of dwelling on Cheltenham's Pump Rooms and pleasure grounds the newer guide-books drew attention to 'the variety of places of worship, supplied with faithful and eloquent pastors – to its large educational establishments – to its libraries and reading rooms, and to the advantages which its vicinity affords for studying the sciences of Geology and Botany'. Eighteenth-century frivolity had given way to the earnestness and sobriety that was to characterize public expression in the reign of the new young Queen.

In the seventeen years between the building of Underwood's Holy Trinity to accommodate the overflow from St Mary's and the construction of the fashionable Christ Church three further Anglican churches were erected. St James's in Suffolk Square, in 'Churchwarden Perpendicular', was begun by Edward Jenkins but finished by the great Papworth. Papworth himself designed St John's for the wealthy residents of the houses north-east of the High Street, but this was shortly pulled down to be rebuilt in fashionable Gothic. These churches were paid for by their congregations in return for guaranteed sittings and those who had not subscribed had to pay a shilling at the door. It was Francis Close, first a curate at Holy Trinity and then incumbent of St Mary's, still on an official stipend of £40 a year with the present of a new hat thrown in, and still designated Perpetual Curate, who rebelled against this discrimination. He persuaded Cheltenham to subscribe, and the Government to grant £3000 to build the 'Free Church of St Paul's' designed by Forbes of the Pittville Pump Room, north-west of the High Street, at the poor end of the town.

Close had been chosen by the Simeon Trust for his Evangelical sentiments. In the thirty years before he was translated to be Dean of Carlisle he waged war against Colonel Berkeley, now created Earl Fitzhardinge and Baron Segrave, and all he stood for. Berkeley managed to survive until 1857, a year after Close departed to the North, when he ended his life appropriately after a fall from his horse while hunting, but there was little doubt that the clergyman gained the ascendancy. Tennyson, who came to St James's Square in the 1840s had a particular abhorrence for the Evangelicals, and was shortly to utter his famous description of Cheltenham – the 'polka, parson-worshipping place'. The Berkeleys were Whigs, but, for all his championship of the poor, as far as their right to a seat in church went, Close was solidly Tory. He was also courageous. 'In my humble opinion,' he declared at a meeting of the Working Men's Association, 'the Bible is Conservative, the Prayer Book is Conservative, the Church Conservative, it is impossible for a minister to open his mouth without being a Conservative.' Only a year after his appointment the thirty-year-old minister was challenging aristocratic prejudice in a sermon against the races. These had become an annual three-day event with all manner of profane entertainment in a fair beside the course. Close's diatribe was printed, 3500 copies of it, provoking a war of pamphlets and the fury of the Berkeley faction and the many Roman Catholic Irish living in the town. Though he never succeeded in stamping out horse-racing

Close was undaunted by hostility. He lived to be described as 'the Cheltenham Gamaliel – and emphatically the great man of the place. Monarch of all he surveys in that resort of fashion, and never did Beau Nash rule with more absolute supremacy. The authorities of the town sink into insignificance when their influence is placed beside that of the potent Vicar.' The 'merriest sick resort on earth' came to be nicknamed 'Close Borough', growing always more sedate and sober.

Other objects of the parson's attack were alcohol, Popery and Puseyism, and the theatre. It appeared an Act of God when, at 4 a.m. on 3 May 1839, Watson's little Theatre Royal which had accommodated George III and employed the greatest names in theatrical history, caught fire and burned to the ground. The spectacle was as dramatic as any seen upon its stage. There was not a breath of wind, so 'the stationary appearance of the flames' resembled 'an enormous fire purposely enclosed within four walls, whence they shot up in a continued and overwhelming column, of intense brilliancy and fearful beauty. One by one the ponderous beams fell in, myriads of sparks clustered above the high and sparkling beacon of ruins. So intense was the action of the fire, that no single article could be saved; – everything perished; – pit, gallery, boxes, ceiling, stage, scenery, dresses, properties, books, music.' The fact that the flames did not spread to the adjoining houses, despite the late arrival of the fire engines, added to the impression of heavenly intention, and Close gained extra satisfaction from the knowledge that a great deal of expense had recently gone on redecorating and repairing what was now a heap of ashes. No other cause than divine wrath could be discovered, for the footlights and chandeliers had been extinguished in the presence of the manager at 11 p.m. the previous night. Close's influence prevented its being rebuilt, and there was now no permanent theatre. Occasional plays and concerts were given, despite Evangelical protest, in the Assembly Rooms and at the Royal Well Music Hall built by Samuel Onley on the site of Skillicorne's Long Room. Cheltenham's Pope did not have it all his own way, for when Fanny Kemble came to give a Shakespeare reading she managed to draw a fuller house than he did, though he mounted a rival attraction in a lecture entitled 'The Tendencies of the Stage, Religious and Moral'.

Another object of the future Dean's displeasure was the railway. Not only did he preach against that popular clerical target, Sunday trains, but against rail travel in general. With other Cheltenham parsons he was particularly opposed to the project to build a line to London through Northleach, Witney, Aylesbury and Tring, a plan which involved bringing the new steaming monsters dangerously near a number of churches and chapels.

Cheltenham was untouched by the railway age until 1835, though communications with the outside world had improved since the days of the Gloucester Flying Machine and its three-day journey. A fast coach left the Plough every morning to reach London in ten and a half hours; others ran to Birmingham, Liverpool and Bath. About forty coaches rattled along the High Street every day, to and fro to Exeter, Coventry, Wolverhampton, Manchester, Sheffield and Chester. When the possibility of a railway was mooted two rival projects were offered by two rival companies. To the satisfaction of the clergy the line through Tring was never built, but the other concern called in Brunel to plan a route by way of Gloucester and Stroud to join the Great Western line from London to Bristol near Swindon. Money ran short and Cheltenham's first railway was constructed along the route of the old horse-tramway to Gloucester, on which, for some time, coal trucks continued to be pulled. This became part of the Birmingham–Gloucester line, starting from Lansdown Station. Even something so utilitarian as a railway station was then thought worthy of a Grecian portico, and Daukes designed a handsome one supported on twelve Doric columns. It was another five years before the journey to London could be made direct. The Great Western Railway bought up the Gloucester–Stroud–Swindon company and in 1845 opened a new terminus in St James's Square, joined to Lansdown by a line a mile and a quarter long. Within a few years stage coaches had vanished from the streets, and some of the inns from whose yards they started went out of business.

But Close's influence was not wholly destructive. While

busily campaigning against the pastimes of the fading Spa he was ambitiously transforming it into a centre for pious learning. As Anglican churches sprang up on all sides he helped to lay the foundations of a number of places of education, careful that they bore the stamp of the Evangelical movement. In the year that his anti-rail propaganda was frustrated he had the compensation of seeing the Cheltenham Proprietary College founded, the first new public school of Victoria's reign. Ironically, its success had a good deal to do with the town's improving communications.

The College was conceived in 1840 when a committee of thirty-six shareholders, as exclusive as the membership of the Assembly Rooms, was floated – 'no person to be considered eligible who should not be moving in a circle of gentlemen. No retail trader being under any circumstances to be considered.' Lord Sherborne was President; Francis Close and the Reverend J. Browne of Holy Trinity Vice Presidents. The founders had strong Anglo-Indian connections, and the preparation of boys for the Army and Indian Civil Service was a prime consideration. The school opened in the following year with the Reverend Albert Phillips, D.D., as Principal. At a ceremony in the Assembly Rooms the clergy appeared in 'full canonicals', the 120 boys carrying their 'collegers' or mortarboards which, it was hoped, would compel them to behave like little gentlemen in the streets. 'It is only the folly of shallow philosophers and modern republicans that would strip off these distinctions. It was the wisdom of our ancestors which clothed our judges in ermine, our peers in their robes, our counsellors and clergy in their gowns; and he was little skilled in human nature who attached no importance to such things.' This, from Close's sermon, was characteristic. The school prepared boys for the universities, but he deplored the effect that study of the classics, compulsory for entrance, might have. 'Every pious parent must feel that there is great peril in putting into the hands of youth the abominable mythology of the ancients, tending as it did to warp their understandings, and to destroy their better feelings. It is painful to think that a classical education could not be acquired without the use of such works;

but how can this baneful tendency be so effectually neutralized as by constant and pious inculcation of Christian truths?'

The school began in two houses in the middle of Bayshill Terrace, 'within 200 yards of the grand Promenade, the locality [being] as nearly centrical as could reasonably be hoped for'. The fifty boarders paid £35 a year and had a horse-hair mattress, a feather bolster and a pillow. There were seventy day-boys or half-boarders. The opening was celebrated at the Queen's Hotel, where dinner for the seventy-eight proprietors, though copious and elegant, was characteristic of all Close had a hand in – 'there were no toasts'.

In 1843 another sedate dinner at the Queen's Hotel celebrated the completion of the present building, of Tudor Gothic style with two oblong schoolrooms, 'Big Classical' and 'Big Modern' on either side of a central tower. Simultaneously the contractor and his workmen sat down to roast beef and plum pudding in the school hall. Whatever the directors may have done, they did not scruple to drink the school's success 'with three times three and the Kentish fire'.

Outwardly all appeared prosperous; internally the school was far from satisfactory. The boarding-houses lacked baths and water-closets; their inmates' clothes were filthy. Most of the discipline was administered by 'drivers', assistants to the house-masters, whose business was to herd the boys, outside lesson times, into playgrounds fenced with six-foot railings and see they stayed there out of the way of the staff. There was the usual Victorian bullying, with 'roastings' in the *Tom Brown* manner; there were complaints that games of 'Hare and Hounds' broke farm fences and disturbed cattle. Three years after the school had opened 144 boys had been removed by shocked and angry parents, and it was not till Dr Phillips had been replaced by William Dobson of Trinity, Cambridge, that its fortunes took a turn for the better. Dobson was a man of humour and good temper who genuinely liked boys and refused to force Evangelical principles upon them.

Close was also instrumental in setting up a Sunday school for infants, subsequently converted into a day school. By 1844 he had started five others, all dedicated to combating Tractarian influence at the earliest possible moment in a child's life. The fifty boys from the Charity School, which still met in the tiny room over the porch of St Mary's, were moved to new premises in Devonshire Street. To continue his work Close needed teachers, trained upon 'Scriptural, Evangelical, and Protestant principles', and, in 1849, St Paul's Training College was founded in another Gothic building by Daukes in the poor quarter of the town near the free church of that name. This was followed by the creation of the sister college of St Mary, for women students, in St George's Place.

Close was also the moving spirit on the 'Vestry Committee of resolute men' who met to rescue the ancient Grammar School from the neglect into which it had fallen. The Fellows of Corpus Christi had been no more conscientious in carrying out Pate's intention for the school than they had been in administering his alms-houses. Though the value of Trust property was continually increasing the headmaster had been paid no more in 1815 than the £16 allotted in Queen Elizabeth's reign. The stipend had been raised to £30 the next year, a sum still insufficient to attract a man who had to be an M.A. Pupils had been asked to pay for subjects other than Greek and Latin, and their numbers had fallen to thirty-four. The Committee decided that 'the charities appear of late years to have wholly failed of their original intentions'. They accused Corpus Christi of mismanagement and misappropriation and eventually after wasting more Trust income on litigation, the Fellows were persuaded to agree to their demands. Pate's old stone building was closed in 1848, to be opened four years later with a new system of teaching, an additional schoolroom and a new headmaster. By the time Close left for Carlisle there were 150 scholars and a waiting-list of as many more.

Strangely enough Close does not seem to have been at the meeting in September 1853 which laid the foundation of the most widely celebrated of Cheltenham's schools, though he was elected its President. In the house of the Reverend H. Walford Bellairs, Inspector of Schools for Gloucestershire, a discussion took place upon the setting up of a 'Proprietary College for the education of young ladies' and to 'afford a first rate education to the Daughters and young children of Noblemen and Gentlemen' in 'Holy Scripture and the Liturgy of the Church of England, the principles of Grammar, Geography, History, Arithmetic, French, Music, Drawing and Needlework'. Mrs Proctor, a colonel's widow, was chosen Principal, though the acting head was her daughter, Anne. Cambray House, where Wellington had stayed in 1816, was the College's first premises, with an added schoolroom, 30 feet by 40 feet. There was a pleasant garden running down to the Chelt, two rustic bridges and an old apricot tree, laden with fruit in a good season. Close does not seem to have concerned himself much in the early struggles of the school, which, for the first four years, before its second headmistress was appointed, went through growing pains similar to those which beset the boys' College.

It was not only schools and churches that were built in the first half of Victoria's reign. In 1844 the town could boast '56 bakers; 88 grocers; 50 butchers; 173 licensed victuallers; 43 libraries and stationers; 167 milliners and dressmakers; 300 lodging house keepers; 80 medical men; 30 chemists'. The age of shopping as a pastime had begun, with Cavendish House, established in 1818 in the Promenade by a local company, and the attractive Montpellier Walk, a row of shops of the kind inseparable from a tourist resort, 'milliners, pastrycooks and circulating libraries' on either side of the Rotunda. Between these, instead of pillars, armless plaster statues had been inserted – 'female figures clothed in long garments, and called by the Greeks, Caryatides'. Though the drapery was voluminous it was revealing and it cannot be imagined that these celebrated ladies gave pleasure to Cheltenham's 'Pope', who disliked classical architecture as much as he deplored its literature, preferring the religiously inspired Victorian Gothic.

The Queen's Hotel, in which the College founders had their banquets, was also classical, and had been opened in 1838 on the site of the removed Imperial Spa, forming a new termination to the Promenade. Apart from the hospital, built ten years later, it was the town's last imitation temple, copied by Jearrad from Jupiter's in Rome, with a portico of six Corinthian pillars. At a cost of £40,000 it contained 70 bedrooms and 16 sitting-rooms, with 30 rooms for servants and ample stabling for gentlemen's horses. It supplanted the Clarence, previously the resort of royalty and now the Police Station, as the grandest hotel in town.

Scott's magnificent Thirlestaine House had been suggested as a lodging for William IV for a projected visit that never took place. It was bought by Lord Northwick on the death of its first owner. This eccentric bachelor had amassed a fine collection of Holbeins, Titians and Poussins, some of which he housed in Northwick Place near Broad Campden. He built wings on either side of Thirlestaine House to serve as galleries and opened them free of charge, taking pleasure in conducting visitors himself, explaining the difference between one school of painting and another. The town had hopes of acquiring this splendid collection, but Northwick died intestate and it had to be dispersed. The house was then bought by Sir Thomas Phillipps, who filled the galleries with manuscripts and books. Standing next to Cheltenham College, it now forms part of the school.

By this time the streets, at least in theory, were lit by gas, piped along the High Street by a private company in 1818. An Act of 1821 gave the Commissioners the right to build a gasometer, but, as in many civic matters, they were in no hurry, and, while they hesitated, another private company erected a gasworks on the bank of the Chelt west of the High Street. The inefficient sewerage was due to these same authorities. Jenner had designed town sewers as long ago as 1808, but little had been done to implement his plans, and it was not till 1834 that inadequate arrangements were made, again by private enterprise. In the matter of water the Commissioners were little more efficient, spending their time in unsuccessful attempts to compel William Barrett of the Cambray Mill to carry out his obligation to let the river run down the High Street. In 1824 another private company built a reservoir on Hewlett's Hill to supply those who could pay for it. While disputes continued the water shortage caused a dangerous situation, especially in cases of fire. The making of pavements, for which, with lighting and cleaning, the Commissioners had first been appointed, had been taken out of their hands by the Act of 1821, after which it was the duty of each separate householder to 'pave the footway and stone the road to the centre' in front of his property. Once this was done it was the Vestry's duty to maintain the surface, the cleaning only being left to the Commissioners.

Having failed to provide the town with water, light or sewers, these gentry, with a passion foreshadowing the bureaucrats of the next century, devoted their energy to the frustration of anyone who desired to park a vehicle, drawing up complicated regulations and exacting exorbitant fines. Owners of anything from a sedan chair to a hackney carriage had to be licensed, each driver's uniform to be marked with a registration number three inches high. He might not stir from his vehicle while awaiting fares. As new forms of transport were invented so were new restrictions, until, in 1827, the drivers were compelled to strike. The magistrates found these regulations absurd, as well as other by-laws, such as one forbidding tradesmen to carry baskets over footways after 10 a.m., and refused to convict those brought before the courts for their infringement. Of the fifty Commissioners, many never bothered to attend meetings, and their unpopularity deepened, the more so as they had not been elected and held their discussions in secret. Joseph Pitt did not consider his new town as part of Cheltenham and Thomas Billings saw no reason why the Commissioners should be allowed to levy rates on his Park Estate. Attempts to define the town boundaries led to vast expense and scenes of indescribable confusion at Parish meetings. The Commissioners' offer to have themselves elected led to further acrimony, since only ratepayers were eligible, more than one vote falling to landlords and none at all to the poor. The proposal was defeated by the vested interests of Pitt and Billings and the Liberal supporters of the Berkeleys. The only results of the battle were that Cheltenham had fourteen more years of inefficient government and that Bayshill and Pittville escaped the payment of rates.

After the Reform Bill of 1832 Cheltenham had its first Member of Parliament since Elizabeth I had excused the town the expense of sending a representative to Whitehall. In spite of

Close, Pitt and other influential Conservatives, the Honourable
Craven Berkeley, youngest brother of the Colonel, was returned
unopposed as Liberal member. Cheltenham, which managed
to acquire a reputation for stuffy Conservatism, was in fact, for
many years, an unshaken Liberal stronghold. This triumph for
the Berkeleys and their supporters – the Nonconformists, the
tradespeople, the middle and lower classes – was celebrated
with 'hilarity, good humour and excellent singing' at a dinner
at the Sussex Arms. The Plough, the Assembly Rooms, the
Fleece and Swan were decorated, and a procession with flags
proclaiming 'Berkeley and Independence' was notable for the
absence of the gentry and their horses. The unusual plaster
statue of William IV in Montpellier Gardens was not, as its
inscription oddly states, put up to celebrate this Bill, but was,
in fact, erected to mark his accession to the throne.

The population of Close's parish had doubled during his
ministry, with a startling increase in collections. Voluntary
offerings brought the official stipend of £40 to something
approaching £1200 a year. In 1838 the congregation clubbed
together to build a house – The Grange – as a present to him
and his heirs, and when he left for Carlisle in 1856 there was
grief and mourning, especially among the ladies. He was
showered with gifts – a clock, a silver tea-service, a folio bible –
and many proofs of esteem.

It was as well that Close departed when he did. He might
otherwise have found himself baptizing a child, the next year,
whose subsequent career would have been anathema to him.
Two or three hundred yards from St Mary's churchyard, in a
room above a stable, Fred Archer was born – destined to be the
greatest English jockey until Gordon Richards broke his record
in the next century. His father was a notable steeplechase-rider
and young Fred was horse mad. He lost his first race on a pony
at Prestbury and came home in tears. He went on, however, to
win 2748 races; the Derby five times, the Oaks four, the St
Leger six and the 2000 Guineas five times. At the age of twenty-
nine he shot himself, certainly not for debt, for he left £66,662.
Racing enthusiasts, in search of his birthplace should be warned
that the memorial plaque has almost certainly been affixed to

the wrong house. All the evidence, in title deeds and birth certificates, belongs in a pleasant little house, converted from the cottage and adjoining stable, which backs on Rowland Hill's derelict chapel's graveyard. It is situated at the end of a narrow alleyway immediately behind the house in St George's Place that bears the plaque.

In the year of Fred Archer's birth a character who would have appreciated him, Colonel Berkeley, Earl Fitzhardinge, came near to making his peace with God before dying from the effects of his fall in the hunting field. Dean Close had no hand in the conversion. As a prominent Liberal Berkeley was obliged to make a show of toleration and, in 1852, had helped the Congregationalists to build a new place of worship in Winchcombe Street, Highbury Chapel having grown too small for them. Their minister, like many Nonconformists, was a Whig, both politically and religiously an opponent of Close. Also a fearless man, and a great harvester of souls, Dr Morton Brown did not scruple to tackle his lordly benefactor, one of the last of the Regency rakes, on the subject of his other-worldly future, before accepting his money.

'My Lord, there is one thing I should like to say to you, as a minister of Christ, before we separate.'

'What is that?'

'I would remind you that you have yourself a soul to be saved or lost.'

'Thank you, Morton Brown, I hope some time or other to have a long talk with you on the subject.'

They did not meet again for several years, but after the accident it was Berkeley who sent for Brown and, according to the minister, they had no less than seventy-five discussions at the Earl's bedside, Brown shouting down a trumpet into Berkeley's ear. The minister did not conceal his satisfaction at having brought so notable a sinner to repentance and Cheltenham heard the details in two funeral orations, remarkable for their lack of decent reticence. The Colonel's last speeches were made, however, to his favourite hounds, which were sent for to his deathbed. 'They were probably the beings he loved most on earth.'

CHAPTER TEN

The Cheltenham Ladies

THE standard apricot tree in the garden of Cambray House was thickly covered with fruit in 1858, the summer in which the Ladies' College acquired a new headmistress. The girls' school had got off to a start as bad as that made by the Proprietary College. Discipline had been slack, with dog fights punctuating morning classes, for pets were allowed to be kept in the cloakroom; there had been arguments between the Proctors and the Council. The original hundred pupils had dwindled to sixty-nine in five years; the capital from £2000 to £400. When the Principals resigned there were fifty applicants for the headship, and the one that carried the day was a twenty-seven-year-old woman with a high forehead, smooth light brown hair and what were described as 'wonderful eyes with their calm outlook and their expression of vision'. Normally confining herself to dresses of grey or brown, Dorothea Beale borrowed a striking blue frock for the interview, an impulse which demonstrated, for once in her life, a faint lack of confidence in herself and her own determination to be austere. She had reason to be nervous. She brought a reputation for High Church sympathies which might have damned her in the eyes of the Evangelicals who continued to dominate Cheltenham even after their Pope had departed to Carlisle. Miss Beale had been dismissed from her post as head teacher at Casterton, the Calvinist school that had given Charlotte Brontë a model for 'Lowood', for alleged Tractarian sentiments. Its incumbent's testimony to her 'high sense of duty, and inflexible integrity of principle, and conscientious following of the path of duty regardless of consequences' sounded more like a warning than a commendation.

Miss Beale managed to persuade the Council that her belief in 'Baptismal Regeneration' was not a dangerous heresy.

The famous rhyme

> Miss Buss and Miss Beale
> Cupid's darts do not feel.
> How different from us
> Miss Beale and Miss Buss.

has been responsible for fixing two errors in the minds of successive generations – the first that Miss Buss, a London pioneer of women's education, was co-principal of Cheltenham Ladies' College, where, in fact, she never visited; the second, that Dorothea Beale had never loved, a statement she was at pains to deny. She had been engaged but had broken the contract. All that is known of this episode is her remark that 'no sorrow is greater than the discovery that someone we loved was unworthy'. At fifty she was again to reject marriage, admitting that there was 'some vanity, perhaps, in the refusal'. Her work in Cheltenham had given her a name throughout the English-speaking world and she may be forgiven for wishing to die with it. She often spoke of the Ladies' College as her 'husband'.

The new Principal was faced with an uphill struggle. Her ideas on teaching, fostered at Queen's College, London, a place of higher education for women where Miss Buss had also studied, were ahead of Cheltenham parents, who only wanted their daughters groomed to catch good husbands. She tried to be tactful, introducing learned subjects gradually, but even arithmetic was suspect. Mothers feared that knowledge would turn their girls into boys. 'It is all very well for my daughter to read Shakespeare, but don't you think it is more important for her to be able to sit down at the piano and amuse her friends?' Exams were frowned on; it was difficult to get adequate teachers. Money was short, economies vital, and, in spite of the '43 libraries and stationers', there appears to have been no decent bookshop in the town. 'I went into one of the principal shops and asked for *The Idylls of the King* which had just been published. I was answered, "We have never had any poetical effusions in the library, and we don't think we shall begin now" ' – this in a place where Tennyson, recently created Poet

Laureate, had lived for six years and written most of *In Memoriam.*

Miss Beale remained undaunted. She enforced a rule of silence broken only for twenty minutes each morning. She deplored the Victorian habit of fainting and encouraged self-criticism, applying the rules to herself as well as her charges. Her diaries were full of admonitions to herself – 'more earnestness in work needed'; 'fresh resolutions against the spirit of indolence'; 'again a quarter of an hour wasted'; 'neglect of prayer. Several times rude.' As she grew older she became autocratic, and teachers complained they could not call their souls their own, but she was said never to be sarcastic. She was not one to turn her back on any aspect of life and did not shrink from having her senior girls taught Latin, but Close would have approved her remark that 'one needs to have one's moral fibre braced by the poetry of the Hebrews, and of England and Germany, if one would remain unaffected by writings saturated with heathen thought'. The idea of bracing the moral fibre of girls was new and was to change the pattern of female education.

At the end of her first year only £40 was left in the bank and the lease of Cambray House was up, but with the appointment of J. Houghton-Brancker as auditor fortunes took a turn for the better. A yearly tenancy was negotiated and in the next ten the pupils rose to over 150. A boarding-house was opened in Lansdown Road, but more accommodation was soon needed and in 1870 Fauconberg House was bought – not the house occupied by George III which had been pulled down and rebuilt as Bays Hill House for Baron de Ferrières – but another of the same name in the grounds of the Old Well. The Council was persuaded to borrow money to buy more Well land for a new school building, but its members threatened to resign if Cambray was vacated. Dr Jex-Blake, Principal of Cheltenham College changed their minds, declaring that 'teachers so able and energetic and successful have a right to the greatest consideration, and the very best arrangements'. John Middleton designed a building of ecclesiastical appearance costing £5000, which was thought absurdly grandiose, but numbers were soon up to 220. The school moved, not without regret at leaving the pleasant house where Wellington had stayed, in 1873. From that time onwards, even after Miss Beale's death, it never ceased to expand, becoming one of the most powerful influences in the battle for women's education, and, at the present time, the largest girls' boarding-school in the world. Its spreading premises swallowed all that remained of Skillicorne's beautiful Well Walk, which had, in any case, lost its importance since the parallel development of the Promenade. Now nothing is left to commemorate his historic design except the name Royal Well on the street that runs, between Royal Crescent and the Promenade, from the Ladies' College to the parish church. Miss Beale's attitude to the school's expansion was summed up in her reply to a visiting examiner who, trying to break an awkward silence at a luncheon, remarked, 'I see your buildings are nearing completion'. 'Completion', said Miss Beale annihilatingly, 'means death.'

Ten years before the Ladies' College moved to its permanent site, when its pupils were sitting their first exams before Oxford lecturers, John Goding published his massive *Norman's History of Cheltenham*. Goding had sat with Close on the Vestry Committee that persuaded Corpus Christi to do the right thing by the Grammar School. His book paid tribute to the Perpetual Curate's influence on the town's education, but he did not mention the work of Miss Beale. It was not yet obvious that Cheltenham was the scene of a startling new departure in women's emancipation. Goding's book listed the churches which had been built in the thirty-three years between Close's arrival and its publication. 'Eight edifices, mostly of a spacious and expensive character, have been erected and consecrated according to the rites of the Established Church.' These included the five mentioned earlier – Holy Trinity (1826), St James's and St John's (1829), St Paul's (1831), and the handsome and fashionable Christ Church (1840), with its impressive tower a prominent feature of the Cheltenham skyline. To these were added St Philip's, near the Park; St Luke's, off the Bath Road south of Sandford Park, built largely from small subscriptions by the poorer people; and the most remarkable in appearance, the pseudo-Norman St Peter's, designed by Daukes in 1849. This massive building, with its central lantern, looks imposingly solid, but its great round pillars resound hollowly when struck, being made of flimsy plaster. St Peter's was in a slum parish which had sprung up near the gasworks, a place where 'people of respect are afraid to live.... Persons are stoned and pelted with mud . . . one or two have lost their lives.' All these churches kept their worship low enough to satisfy the Evangelicals, though services at Christ Church inclined discreetly towards the cathedral type, and those of All Saints were 'ornate and full' without being Ritualistic. For Ritualism, said the guide-books smugly, one had to go as far as Prestbury.

Whatever Close had done to stimulate the building of new churches, he seems to have turned a blind eye to the deterioration of the fabric of his own, in spite of the size of his congregation and the largesse they dropped in the plate. St Mary's was the oldest building in a town now largely Regency and Victorian, the only relic of pre-Reformation Cheltenham. With the fees from baptisms, marriages, burials and the erection of monuments the value of the living was now about £700. Close was succeeded by the Reverend E. Walker, a tablet in the church to whose memory reads, 'by the purchase of the chancel, February 19th, 1863, he became the first Rector of Cheltenham'.

He arrived to a sea of troubles. The letting of pews had been discontinued the year before, and the consequent rearrangement of sittings led to the unpleasant discovery that the vaults under the south aisle were gaping open to reveal coffins and the foundations of the pillars supporting the galleries were unsound. The church was immediately closed. Two possibilities were open – to pull down St Mary's, leaving the town with no memorial to its monastic origins, and build another church on the site; or to house the congregation in a temporary building till the galleries could be removed, the vaults and graves filled in and covered with concrete, and the whole fabric made safe. After much argument and an appeal to the Home Secretary, an Order in Council was obtained to preserve the ancient church, the townspeople, including many Nonconformists, rallying round to collect money for the work.

In the meantime a temporary church was put up where Mrs Field's Boarding House of Georgian fame had stood. With its corrugated iron 'fluted and painted stone colour' and its little spire 'a passer-by who knew nothing of its history would not suppose that it was intended for a mere temporary structure'. The congregation became attached to its new place of worship and £20,000 was subscribed for a permanent chapel of ease on the site. The temporary church was moved to Bayshill so that the vast St Matthew's could be built there. It was opened in 1879 with room for 1450 worshippers. The next Rector, Canon Bell, had the strange wish to make this severe, unfriendly building into the parish church, but he met with such opposition that he was forced to abandon the idea, and St Matthew's was kept for its original purpose. The old church reopened with the unsightly galleries removed, the quaint three-decker pulpit and the family pews destroyed, a repaired roof, new heating and lighting. A south porch had been added to eliminate draught and the north porch, with its historic schoolroom, opened to the body of the church and made into the Baptistery. To complete the transformation new glass was needed and was provided by three eminent townsmen, James Agg-Gardner, Baron de Ferrières and W. H. Gwinnett. The restoration was unfortunate in being carried out in the middle of Victoria's reign for the resulting glass, gaudy and glowing with colour in the taste of the period, obscures the window tracery and makes the interior dark and gloomy.

St Matthew's added a ninth Anglican church to the eight recorded by Goding. Two others had been added in the 1860s; All Saints' and St Mark's – the latter due to become the centre of a vast new housing-estate near the Gloucester Road in the next century. The Dissenters had also been industriously building. Samuel Onley's Congregational chapel in Winchcombe Street, largely paid for by Colonel Berkeley, stood for eighty years, when it was taken down to make room for a cinema. The Baptists possessed three chapels in Cheltenham – Bethel in St James's Square, Cambray in Regent Street and Salem in Clarence Parade. Wesley's followers had increased only slowly after his visits and met amid ridicule and persecution in a rented house in Albion Street, but by 1812 they had collected enough money to build Ebenezer Chapel in King Street, and when this became too small another in Bath Street. In spite of Goding's optimistic reports, Quakers in Cheltenham seem to have suffered as much as anywhere before the Toleration Act of 1889. Their Meeting House, with the cemetery where Elizabeth Skillicorne was buried, was in Grove Street, till they moved in 1836 to a larger room in Manchester Street. The Unitarians took over their building until they were able to build their Anglo-Norman church in Royal Well Place.

The 'Jews and Jewesses' whose presence in the streets offended Cobbett in the 1820s had a small synagogue in Manchester Place. In 1839 they built another in St James's Square and acquired a burial ground in Elm Street. Their congregation was flourishing, with a number of wealthy residents and shopkeepers, but in 1874 the building was closed for want of money, to be reopened only in the twentieth century.

Apart from the Anglican churches the largest was the Roman Catholic St Gregory, consecrated in 1857 to replace the chapel built for refugees in 1810. It marked a new era of toleration for its people. Catholics had been in danger in Close's reign, especially when his annual anti-papal diatribe stirred Protestants to fever pitch on Guy Fawkes Day. Attempts had been made to set fire to the old church in 1850, when passions ran high after the division of the country into territories under Roman Catholic bishops. Failing to destroy the building, the enraged Protestants turned their wrath on Catholic-owned shops. Peace was restored after St Gregory's was built. In the Gothic style, with a spire not unworthy to stand so near the ancient one belonging to St Mary, the church was served by Benedictines, who had long connections with Gloucestershire, having built Gloucester Cathedral and Tewkesbury Abbey.

With all these places of worship and no theatres 'the merriest sick resort on earth' was changed indeed in the three-quarters of a century since George III's visit, and Goding deplored the lack of entertainment since the burning of the Theatre Royal. Plays were sometimes staged in the Assembly Rooms, but the only approach to a replacement was Samuel Onley's Royal Well Music Hall. On a stage with a drop curtain painted with a view of Lake Como were presented concerts, amateur plays and dramatic readings such as those of Fanny Kemble. Unlike Close, Goding believed 'the theatre, in a reformed state, would . . . be an important and highly influential school of morality' and regretted that 'a town surrounded with a population of 50,000 should not possess a temple wherein the tragic muse might be celebrated', fearing that 'the gloomy state of society, without pleasurable entertainment, will invariably lead to drunkenness and infidelity' – a prophecy which proved, by the end of the century, to be only too accurate.

Ignoring the existence of brothels in the slums, the newer guide-books smugly pointed to a life altered out of recognition from that described in Moreau's editions. 'The town is no longer a type of fashionable watering place. . . . The frivolities once so prevalent here are now more honoured in the breach than the observance. . . . Education has also powerfully done its work for good in Cheltenham. The gross and vicious habits of a past generation have fled or died out before the spread of education and intelligence, and a comparatively healthy moral tone now permeates all classes. Occasionally a character of the old stamp may appear on the fashionable horizon . . . but he is carefully avoided and excluded from family circles.' Cheltenham even managed to earn golden opinions from the Scots for its observance of the Sabbath – 'better kept in Cheltenham than anywhere else in Britain – outside Scotland'. Francis Close had left his influence behind him.

While the townsmen's spiritual needs were amply provided for, their earthly requirements, the province of the unpopular Commissioners, were less efficiently supplied. Of the street lamps, 273 were out of action in the 1870s because of a shortage of gas, and those that still functioned had their time of lighting cut to save money, with consequent risk to life and limb. The wells were running dry, increasing the danger of fire. Efforts to get water from South Cerney were frustrated by London water companies, anxious for their own supplies, so Cheltenham householders, to their disgust, had to drink from the Severn, which they suspected was polluted by Worcester sewage. The poorer districts could not afford even this questionable supply. Under a private company the sewerage system was wholly inadequate and the Commissioners' new scheme, to tap the Hatherley and Wyman brooks, was almost frustrated by the rapacity of Jesus College, which had once owned the advowson of St Mary's and still possessed land in the town. Thirty Commissioners, equally divided into Whigs and Tories, spent four decades ineffectually trying to acquire sole power over light, water and sewers from the private companies, and the story of their bickerings, procrastinations and penny-pinching methods makes dreary reading. Having failed to provide material comfort for their people, they further defaulted in supplying their intellectual needs. An Act of 1855 provided for a free library and museum if enough rate-payers desired them. There were the inevitable arguments, between the town's many teachers, who favoured cultivating the mind of the working man, and the property-owners, who dreaded revolution if the dangerous ammunition of uncensored books was put into his hands. After acrimonious disputes the matter was allowed to drop and the town did not get its public library till 1888.

It was in 1872, at a meeting of the Liberal Party, that the suggestion was put that the Commissioners and their mismanagement might be replaced by a Mayor and Corporation to everyone's advantage. William Nash Skillicorne (of the family of the Spa's founder) pointed out that smaller towns like Tewkesbury, Gloucester and Worcester had the dignity of a Charter of Incorporation. On this point the Tories were with the Whigs, apart from a few dissenters divided between the parties. Some of the objectors feared the peace of Cheltenham would be gone for ever; others, like Skillicorne, who changed his mind on the subject, feared it would lead to an increase in rates; property-owners objected to the loss of their right to a plural vote. Public opinion, however, won the day. A petition was sent to the Queen, who granted a charter in 1876. Strangely enough the first two mayors were Skillicorne, who had become an objector to the bill, followed by Baron de Ferrières, who had opposed it from the beginning. Each, when they had conceded defeat, turned to and worked selflessly for the new Corporation. De Ferrières, grandson of a Napoleonic general, was a naturalized Englishman and member of the Church of England, who had lived at Bays Hill House since 1860. He came to be one of Cheltenham's most popular aldermen and a benefactor as great as, and a good deal more respectable than, the lamented Colonel Berkeley.

CHAPTER ELEVEN

Salubritas et Eruditio

THE motto for the new Incorporated Borough – it did not get its coat of arms for another eleven years – gives a heading to this chapter. The guide books were still making strenuous efforts to arrest the Spa's decline with their emphasis on its salubrity. Of the erudition there was no doubt. All over the once pleasant site of the Old Well Miss Beale was building like a beaver, ever adding to her little empire till, at the end of the century, she had covered Skillicorne's land with classrooms and gymnasia, as well as dotting the slopes of Lansdown and Bays-hill with boarding-houses and playing-fields. The streets were threaded now, morning, midday and evening with little strings of 'Ladies' coming and going between their lodgings and their classes, for the system still in force of living and eating in separate houses, assembling in school only for study and games, began early. Before her 'Silver Wedding' to the school she thought of as her husband, Dorothea Beale had added a great hall, calisthenics rooms, a sanatorium at Leckhampton, a studio, a music wing and a kindergarten. One of her staff put forward the idea of a special house for seniors wishing to train as teachers, and when Miss Newman died, only a year after her project was launched, the Principal appealed for funds to carry it on. The response enabled her to buy another site on Bayshill, and St Hilda's was built, named after the Abbess of Whitby, patroness of learning and poetry. Some of the money was used to buy three acres in Oxford and, in due course, women from Cheltenham began to invade that stronghold of masculine learning in the daughter college of St Hilda.

At the time of the 'Silver Wedding' numbers had risen to 500.

Celebrations included the presentation of an organ and stained-glass windows. The Guild, an organization of ex-pupils, with its emblem, the daisy, was born. 'One of God's hieroglyphics,' was how Miss Beale, not generally given to sentimental fantasy, described it in a sermon – closed 'an emblem of purity'; open 'the true sunflower . . . that stands ever gazing upwards'.

The entire decoration of her school, in late Victorian taste, was calculated to instil ideas of purity, industry and the excellence of women into its inmates. These were still bound, as at Cambray, to keep silence while they walked its marble corridors, lined with statues of real women – Florence Nightingale, Elizabeth Fry, Hannah More, Jenny Lind; and mythological or literary ones – Electra, Antigone, Alcestis; Isabella, Portia, Cordelia; Beatrice, Grizelda, Una. The windows represented Christ in his dealings with the female sex; Martha and Mary, the daughter of Jairus, the Syro-Phoenician woman. The 'Silver Wedding' by no means put an end to Miss Beale's ambitions; classrooms continued to be added, boarding-houses acquired, further playgrounds opened. In 1889 she purchased Onley's Music Hall, believed to stand over Skillicorne's original spring, and in the next year pulled down this place of profane entertainment to replace it with the many-galleried Princess Hall, called after Tennyson's heroine, at a cost of £21,000. Miss Beale had come a long way since the Governors accused her of extravagance for buying a knife and fork for her own use.

The news of Close's death in 1882 made his regretful admirers anxious to set up a memorial, and nothing seemed so appropriate as the creation of another school – dedicated to the inculcation of Protestant and Evangelical Truths. Four years later £10,000 had been collected and Dean Close Memorial School was opened in Shelburne Road, a mile and a half from the town centre between Hatherley Brook and Lansdown Station. The school, which opened with forty boys, did not aspire to the social glory of Cheltenham College with its emphasis on Army and Civil Service. It put religion first, aiming at a public-school education at the lowest fees consistent with the provision of decent food and an efficient staff. Dr W. H. Flecker, from the

City of London Collegiate School, was the first headmaster. As strongly Evangelical as Close, he wrote jealously that the Ritualists never had any difficulty in obtaining money to improve their schools, but he seems to have been an amiable character without the agressiveness of the man in whose name the school had been founded. After sixteen years he was able to boast that, with two hundred pupils, the school was overflowing.

In the year of the Dean Close foundation Pate's ancient Grammar School was pulled down, depriving the town of its last genuine Elizabethan building. The next year it was replaced by a Victorian version of that period, described as 'having a noble Elizabethan façade, with an embattled tower and space for three to four hundred boys'.

In the decade that Cheltenham received its charter two babies were born, destined to be among the town's most famous sons. In Westall, a Cotswold stone terrace-house facing Montpellier Gardens, the wife of a Quaker gave birth, in July 1872, to Edward Adrian Wilson, whose statue, by the sculptress wife of his friend and commander, Scott of the Antarctic, now stands at the south end of the Promenade. In September, two years later, in a little house in Pittville Terrace, the nervous English wife of a musician of Swedish origin produced a sickly baby, the first of two sons – Gustavus Theodore von Holst.

The childhood of these boys, like their subsequent careers and the way Cheltenham chose to honour or ignore them, could hardly have been more different. By the age of three Wilson had discovered his vocation. He was always drawing, particularly from nature. When his mother, who had an interest in farming, took over The Crippets on Leckhampton Hill, he entered into what was for him a veritable paradise, able to wander alone on land once inhabited by the builders of long barrows, collecting arrowheads and drawing foxes and badgers, birds and butterflies in his meticulous style. He went to Cheltenham College, where the headmasters of his time, Kynaston and James, spoke well of his industry and conduct. The man who was later to be, first, a nearly-despaired-of consumptive, and then the mainstay of Scott's two expeditions, was then described as 'a thin, lithe schoolboy, with close-cut, wavy, dark red

The Montpellier Rotunda as it is today. After descending to 'balls, billiards and bingo' the building was bought by the Borough Council to save it from ruin. In 1962 Lloyds Bank, who had occupied part of the Long Room since 1890, offered to restore the entire building and the Rotunda is now the central banking hall.

The semi-circular building at the Promenade end of Montpellier Walk — the row of shops, separated by caryatids, built on either side of the Montpellier Pump Room and Rotunda.

Cheltenham's Regency buildings have the richest and most varied collection of iron balconies and porches in the country. These houses are in Oxford Street and Oxford Parade.

Early Victorian architecture in the poorer district north of the High Street. Houses in Larput Place and the Sweep's House in Sherborne Street.

Built in 1840 and designed by R. W. Jearrad, Christ Church is one of the most successful Victorian Gothic buildings in the country. Inside it possesses a marvellous collection of Victorian military memorials.

The west side of the Promenade with the Municipal Buildings and the First World War memorial.

The interior of the Parish Church towards the end of Close's incumbency. A year after he left to become Dean of Carlisle, the galleries (which had been erected after George III made Cheltenham fashionable) were pulled down.

St Peter's Church. Designed by Daukes in 1849 in the Norman style. Its massive pillars and huge lantern look impressively solid, but resound hollowly when struck, being made of flimsy plaster.

Cheltenham Ladies' College: Miss Beale and pupils in Lower Hall, 1894.

Cricket on Cheltenham College Ground, where the yearly Gloucestershire Cricket Festival is held and where W. G. Grace made 318 not out in 1876. In the centre background is the chapel, built in 1891, and to the left the original one which was turned into the school museum.

Above: *The Winter Gardens, Cheltenham's Crystal Palace, built in the 1890s to attract the sort of people who went abroad to Carlsbad and Baden. It was pulled down at the start of the Second World War, and its site is now occupied by the Imperial Gardens.*

Left: *Cheltenham is famous for its annual Music and Literature Festivals. A native musician was Gustav Holst. Though short-sighted and asthmatic he was forced to spend hours each day in violin practice which he detested. It was not until he started composing and conducting local choirs that he began to enjoy music-making.*

Modern Cheltenham: above *Cavendish House;* below *The Eagle Star building which dominates the skyline.*

hair, a pair of unusually bright blue eyes, and a half-amused, half-quizzical expression, often turning to a merry smile'.

It is unlikely that he ever met his near-contemporary from the further side of the High Street. The von Holst boys went to the Grammar School. They had a colourful family background, their great-grandfather having been a political refugee from Riga. Their grandfather, Gustavus Valentine, settled in Cheltenham in the 1830s and taught the piano. Each year his young lady pupils gave a musical afternoon in which twenty-four of them would sit at twelve pianos giving 'much pleasure to a select audience by their simultaneous rendering of a classical overture'. The next generation, Gustavus Matthias and Adolphus, were also musicians and teachers, but the character of the elder was too original for a place still dominated by Evangelical thought. He developed into a powerful lady-killer with a train of broken hearts, and finally overreached himself when, according to family tradition, he appeared at a fancy-dress ball without a stitch of clothing – 'an episode that reduced Cheltenham to a horrified silence' and forced him to remove himself to Glasgow.

His younger brother (the composer's father) conducted concerts at the Rotunda. He had a reputation for bad temper, obstinacy and sarcasm. Nevertheless, he persuaded one of his pupils, Clara Lediard, to marry him, but after a short time the constant music-making so affected her nerves that Adolph was obliged to practise on a silent piano. She died when their elder son, Gustavus, was eight. The widower was an incompetent father. He failed to notice his son's need of spectacles or to bother about his asthma and this neglect laid the foundation for Gustav's lifelong ill-health. The delicate boy was forced to spend hours in detested practice of the violin, but, though he was never taught any harmony, his discovery of the poem 'Horatius' at the age of twelve inspired him to his first essay in composition, for chorus and orchestra.

In spite of the misery of ill-health, discomfort at home and continual shortage of money, Holst had time to develop a love of the Cotswolds equal to that of Wilson. His first paid engagements were at Wyck Rissington and Bourton-on-the-Water, where he played the organ and organized choral festivals. To reach these he took to a bicycle, a mode of travel that became such a passion with him that it led to strange excesses in later life, such as taking his beloved machine to explore the deserts of North Africa.

While Wilson was winning golden opinions at the College and von Holst making his first orchestral experiments during English lessons at the Grammar School, the new foundation in memory of Dean Close was sheltering a younger genius, who was to grow up, like the older boys, with a love of Gloucestershire, even in its dampest, foggy, winter moods. Little Roy Flecker – he detested his names Herman Elroy and later altered the first of them to James – was two years old when his father was appointed to the school and his earliest memories were of being taken to shop in the Promenade in his mother's pony carriage, where he learnt to read prematurely from shop signs, and of gazing out of the nursery window over his father's rose garden towards the Cotswolds.

> November Evenings! Damp and still
> They used to cloak Leckhampton Hill,
> And lie down close on the grey plain,
> And dim the dripping window-pane,
> And send queer winds like Harlequins
> That seized our elms for violins
> And struck a note so sharp and low
> Even a child could feel the woe.

But it was an enjoyable woe, romantically indulged from the warm interior of the favourite room of his life, later to become his study, hung with pictures cut from annuals and *Pears Cyclopaedia* and the cage of their pet parrot, where he and his sister revelled in the atmosphere of falling dusk and

> . . . crept about like mice, while Nurse
> Sat mending, solemn as a hearse.

The elms were at the bottom of the school garden with the slope of Leckhampton Hill behind. There was another favourite place. Where Shelburne and Lansdown Roads converge is a railway bridge and, at that time, a signal box. Here the small boy with the oriental face and black hair contrasted with a pair of brilliant blue eyes spent hours at his favourite pastime of watching trains. He made friends with the signalman, who once allowed him to climb on the foot-plate of a Midland engine. Little Roy enjoyed his father's society and after school Dr Flecker often joined his son on the bridge. They stood 'on dark winter afternoons, there to watch the multitude of changing lights on the unseen signal posts, astonishing bits of colour unaccountably starring the sombre evening gloom!'

When he was six Roy was sent to Miss Beale's mixed kindergarten, but he did too well and his mother became anxious that praise might spoil his character, so he was sent to a prep school for boys. At eleven he entered his father's school, delighted at this end to the indignity of being walked to and from his classes with his sister and Nanny. He stayed there till he was sixteen, when his father, who thought he should finish his education under another headmaster, sent him to his own old school – Uppingham.

It was in 1893, the year that Flecker joined Dean Close School, that the twenty-one-year-old von Holst saw the first performance of one of his compositions. *Lansdowne Castle*, an operetta on a local subject, was produced at the Corn Exchange and was 'decidedly a success. The music was said to be tuneful, if somewhat in the style of Sullivan, and although at one point the young composer had shocked the audience by introducing an Anglican chant into the dialogue, on the whole it was considered to show great promise.'

Since its Charter of Incorporation and the demise of the Commissioners conditions had improved in the town, but were by no means perfect. The Medical Officer of Health found much to complain of. Sanitary arrangements were unsatisfactory, even in the best houses; in the outlying districts people still had to rely on inadequate wells. In particular, Dr Thorne was shocked about the nuisance from pigs, people being allowed to keep them in their back gardens even in the centre of the town, a practice he felt injurious to the reputation of a 'great Health Resort . . . which was as bad, in what he had seen today, as some places in the Black Country'. There was need for a proper abattoir, the existing slaughter-house being too near the middle of town. The population, when he made his report, was 45,000, with about 9000 houses built over 4203 acres.

The guide books of the nineties gave a brighter picture, for it is not the function of such publications to be critical. Calling Cheltenham 'The Garden Town of England' they had become less sanctimoniously moral than those of Close's day, reverting, like those of Moreau's, to lyrical description. Apart from the ugly muddle of the once-historic High Street, the unmentioned slums, the fact that St Mary's was now hemmed in by the dreary backs of buildings, and the covering over of an attractive stretch of the Chelt at the foot of the Promenade, the town of the century's end retained a great deal of its Regency charm. The passion for shops had swept away a few beautiful houses on the east of the Promenade and spoiled others with windows at street level, but the centre of the wide thoroughfare, its avenue providing the shade beloved by Victorians, and the relatively unspoilt west side, made it one of the pleasantest centres in the country. In an attempt to attract the sort of people who now went abroad to Carlsbad and Baden the Winter Garden had been opened, a Crystal-Palace-like structure covering the space in front of the Queen's Hotel, now laid out as the Imperial Gardens. There were flower beds planted along the west of the Prom and, at its southern end, in front of the re-erected Pump Room, the Neptune fountain had been added. This rather incongruous monument in a Regency setting had been made by Boulton's, one of the first industries to arrive in Cheltenham, a town which had known little of manufacture before the 1850s apart from its centuries-long brewing of beer. Boulton's, a firm of architectural specialists, was commissioned, in 1891, to provide the many-statued reredos for Cheltenham College's new chapel – an imitation on the outside of King's, Cambridge, built to replace the original one, now turned into the school museum. The College had six hundred pupils now, a number equal to that of the girls under Miss Beale's care.

In front of the College the Cotswolds could still be seen enfolding the town on three sides, and, from Christ Church, there

was an uninterrupted view to the Malvern Hills. 'Not a manufacturing chimney is seen. No polluting smoke veils her graces
. . . she reclines white and easefully on the green plain, and lifts
into the pure sky above her nothing but church spire or schol-
astic tower.'

The writer of the above rejoiced that the Second of Man's
Seven Ages 'with shining morning face' had stepped into the
shoes of dyspepsia and gout, changing the mission of the town.
A visitor from an unspecified manufacturing city, arriving on a
summer afternoon, delightedly observed

> a stream of fashionable people . . . emerging from an enter-
> tainment at the Winter Gardens. The beauty of the whole
> scene will not soon be forgotten. The Promenade in its
> picturesque summer dress. The brilliant assemblage, in the
> glowing colours of June costumes, and the striking appearance
> of the buildings and grounds from which they were issuing,
> contrasted vividly with the scenes just left, and invoked the
> exclamation Grand! . . . Music and sunshine and sylvan
> shadow lend their aid to gladden the social scene.

The breeze of gaiety having effectually dispersed the Close
atmosphere night life had been resumed. There was music from
Herr Lorzing's choir and the Quartett Society; concerts in the
Assembly Rooms and Winter Gardens. But townspeople began
increasingly to deplore the lack of a proper theatre and in
September 1890 the *Chronicle* published a subscription list
revealing a share capital of £6000 to provide one. Frank
Matcham was retained to design it. An enthusiast who devoted
all his life to theatres, he had designed 200 by the time of his
death including the London Hippodrome, Coliseum and
Palladium; the Victoria Palace; the Lyric, Hammersmith, and
most of the theatres belonging to Moss Empires. His particular
innovation was in the development of cantilevered galleries,
unsupported by the pillars which, in most old theatres, blocked
the view from many seats. His attractive little Opera House in
Regent Street cost, in the end, double the subscribed capital,
but it was ready the next year to be opened on 1 October with
a triple bill in which Lily Langtry spoke the following appropriate, but hardly inspired, lines –

Hail sylvan city, for thy vanished stage
With us returns at last – a golden age.
'Tis strange that Thespis hence so long should roam.
Where could he find a more congenial home
Than this broad valley sheltered from all ills
In the broad bosom of the eternal hills,
Where shrines of Faith and Learning greet the eye
Nor fog nor factory smoke pollute the eye?

The little theatre was to be the scene of entertainments varying from Grand Opera to circuses and film shows; its stage to be
trodden by most of the famous actors of the late nineteenth
century – Kendals, Bensons, Grossmiths, most of the Terrys;
Mrs Patrick Campbell, Martin-Harvey, Charles Wyndham,
Ada Reeve, Owen Nares, Henry Ainley.

In an attempt to reinstate Cheltenham as a spa the Borough
Council bought the heavily mortgaged Pittville Pump Room
for £5400. The Montpellier water had for some time been
removed to a little Swiss chalet in the gardens opposite, a green
space which was the scene of much activity – lawn tennis,
archery, football and band music. Only the Rotunda was now
in use, for public balls and receptions, while the whole of
Thompson's Long Room, extending across in front of it was in
occupation by the Worcester City and County Banking Company, who had rented the premises from the Montpellier
Rotunda Company since 1876. This bank was conveyed to
Lloyd's in 1890, but it was not till the next century that they
bought and restored the whole building. Those who preferred
the chalybeate waters of Cambray could obtain them at a
small pump-room on the corner of Rodney Terrace. In 1893
the Corporation also bought the Montpellier Gardens, and
advertised their intention to develop the two great spas 'on lines
similar to those adopted at Continental health resorts', such as
Carlsbad and Baden.

There were many other attractions for visitors. What became
the Cricket Festival began in 1872, when one County match
was played each August on the Cheltenham College ground.
Six years later 'the Cheltenham Week' was started with two
matches, and this continued until 1906, when the number was

increased to three. Gloucestershire was then known as the county of the Graces and, from the beginning, W. G. – one of three black-bearded brothers known as the Three Graces – dominated the County's and, very soon, the country's cricket. In the first Cheltenham County match he took twelve wickets and, in 1876, achieved 318, not out, against Yorkshire. It was in a match near the railway line at Gloucester that W. G. hit the longest ball ever, into the open truck of a passing freight-train which took it on to Bristol – forty miles, but only a six!

In 1900 Grace was succeeded as Captain by the Cheltenham born Gilbert Jessop, a product of the Grammar School and a schoolmaster. A powerful hitter, he drew large crowds, all hoping to see him repeat his famous feat of breaking the clock-face on the fantastic Gothic double-towered pavilion on the College playing-field.

No longer such a target for the clergy, steeplechasing con-tinued at Prestbury, the course a natural amphitheatre at the foot of Cleeve Hill, which brought out the best in a good horse and exposed the weakness of a lesser one, with its energy-sapping uphills and a tricky downhill section near the finish. Cheltenham possessed the only hundred-yard archery-range in the Midlands; the Golf Club on Cleeve Common boasted a hundred members; the Cycling Club had its headquarters at the Royal Hotel. The Cotswold Hunt, until 1815 part of the Berkeley, operated from the Plough and had kennels at Prestbury. Eight other hunts were within reach. This was the time when, in fear of further diminution in water-drinking, the guide books began to advertise Cheltenham as 'The Centre for the Cotswolds', a large section of their pages given up, as nowadays, to views of Chipping Campden, the Slaughters, Bourton-on-the-Water and places as far afield as the Wye Valley and the Forest of Dean.

In 1889 the Free Library had at last been built, after bitter wrangling and the imposition of a penny rate. 'Italian' in style, it stood between St Mary's and St Matthew's in Clarence Street and was opened by Sir Michael Hicks-Beach as church bells rang and the town, obedient to instruction, hung out its flags. Ten years later, through the generosity of de Ferrières,

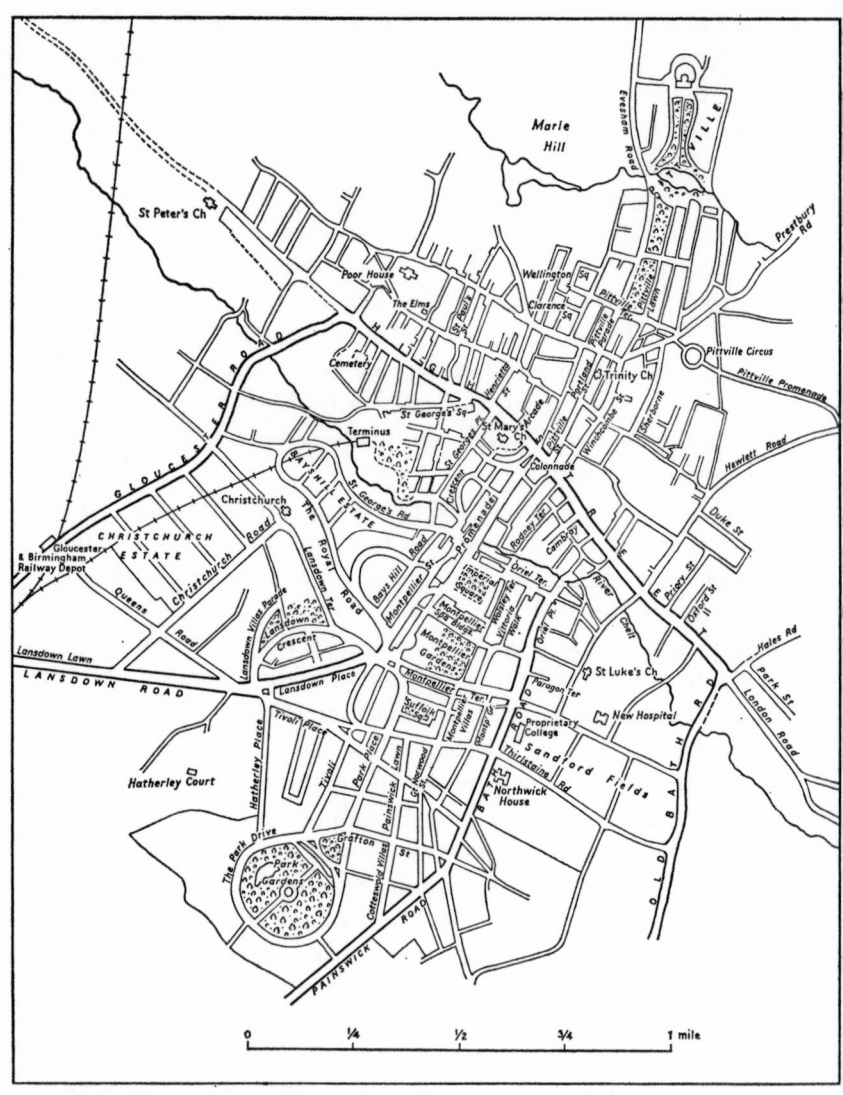

Map after Davies' Survey of 1865, compiled after the construction of the railways and showing the completed Pittville and the large number of new churches.

the Art Gallery was added, with forty of his own Dutch pictures to form a nucleus to the collection.

The first year of the new century saw the destruction of the Assembly Rooms which Wellington had opened in 1816. Lloyd's Bank pulled them down to build their branch in the High Street. The outside had been undistinguished for a Regency building, but the magnificent ballroom was still in use for weekly subscription balls in winter. But these, with concerts and conferences, were soon to have a new venue.

Though the Charter of Incorporation had been granted as long ago as 1876, Cheltenham did not get its Town Hall until 1901, when F. W. Waller's building in the 'Renaissance' style was opened by the Mayor to celebrate the start of Edward VII's reign. Standing between Regent Street and the glass expanse of the Winter Gardens, and next the New Club, built in 1874 and not to be confused with the one that used to meet in the Assembly Rooms, this was now to be the scene of balls and concerts. It also housed a drinking-fountain at which all the various types of Cheltenham water could conveniently be dispensed.

CHAPTER TWELVE

A Town to Let

JUST as the nineteenth century does not properly begin till after Wellington disposed of Napoleon in 1815, the twentieth does not really start till the end of the First World War. In the first nineteen years Cheltenham marked time, continuing as a retiring-place for Army, Navy and Indian Civil Servants, from the prosperous to the genteelly poor. In summer its small hotels profited from an influx of people who spent the winter in resorts like Bournemouth and were driven inland by the increased prices of the bathing season. Outward respectability concealed an area of distress, poverty and unemployment in slums that had arisen in Victorian times, and a degree of prostitution that would have alarmed the visitors. Apart from the brewery, railways and gasworks there were few industrial concerns to provide work, and those mostly small ones.

The guide books continued hopefully to advertise Cheltenham's attractions, but a growing note of desperation was discernible. By the time war came the place was in a state of incipient decay, described as a 'Town to Let'. The schools alone continued to prosper. Several new ones were built, and in 1904, in response to repeated demands, Pate's Grammar School opened a branch for girls at Livorno Lodge. Dorothea Beale, a financial wizard as well as the greatest pioneer of women's education, died in 1906, after nearly fifty years as Principal of the Ladies' College, leaving it the largest and most successful girls' boarding-school in the world, a position it holds to this day. Miss Beale had not approved of competition or rewards. Her successor, Miss Faithfull, relaxed its convent-like discipline to some extent, encouraging outside matches and allowing the girls to compete for prizes and win academic honours.

The war of 1914 was to involve the sons of many families whose names, on the memorial tablets of Cheltenham churches, showed they had already sacrificed a generation to the conflicts of Victoria's reign. The College, with its Army tradition, was destined to be hardest hit, for public schools, with old boys still fresh in the memory and senior ones about to leave, were especially stricken by the decimation of young officers on the fields of France and Flanders.

After the June assassination at Sarajevo not much notice seems to have been taken of the coming storm, for some of the masters were busy planning a yachting holiday in the Baltic by way of the Kiel Canal. But by 4 August the Territorials were ordered to mobilize. So many seniors left before the autumn term that one boarding-house was closed. Scholars increased on the military side, parents 'thinking that their boys were going to be called up for war service and they had better be as well prepared as possible'. Pupils planted the grounds with potatoes. Others made shell-bases, screws and cartridge-punches, earning, at the Armistice, a special commendation from the authorities. Fifteen masters, as well as domestic staff, were at the front. By the end of hostilities 675 old Cheltonians had been killed and 726 wounded and College history records the winning of six V.C.s.

Miss Faithfull offered the Ladies' College to the Red Cross in the event of invasion. This not being called for she converted Eversleigh into a small hospital, each of its wards named after another of the boarding-houses. Convalescent soldiers came to College functions wearing school house ribbons. The girls spent spare time filling sandbags and making comforts for the troops. Daughters of officers killed in action were permitted to remain without charge; children from Belgium were welcomed.

Cheltenham indeed was quickly taken over by the Belgians, for many huge Regency houses were half or wholly empty and put at the disposal of the refugees. The Town to Let had been appropriated by the homeless, the wounded and the convalescent. The newest schools, Naunton Park and Gloucester Road, became hospitals; the big range of buildings on the Prestbury Racecourse were converted to the same use, and a number of mansions on the Cotswolds and private houses in the town given up to the care of the sick. There was also new industry. Not long before the war Boulton's, of the Promenade Fountain (later to make the War Memorial in front of the Municipal Offices) had been joined by a similar small factory for fine wood, metal and stone workers – H. H. Martyn Ltd. This firm, which was to restore the interior of London's Guildhall, the Speaker's Chair and the panelling of the House of Commons, and cast statues for Britain and overseas, now took on important war-work, making, under sub-contract, Nieuport fighter planes at their Sunningend works. This enterprise was to be the start of enormous development in the aircraft industry between Cheltenham and Gloucester.

When the war ended and most of these activities were withdrawn Cheltenham suddenly found itself without aim or purpose. The great houses were empty once more, and in shabbier condition. The 'To Let' signs went up again, with an increasing number of 'For Sale' ones among them, and a four-storey house in beautiful Lansdown Crescent could be bought for as little as £250.

Of the three Cheltenham boys mentioned earlier, only Gustav Holst was alive at the end of the war. Rejected from the forces for short sight and the neuritis that had plagued his infancy, he spent the time in London teaching at Morley College and St Paul's Girls' School. He dropped the *von* from his name when he secured a post to organize music for the Y.M.C.A. in Salonika and was at last allowed to visit the scene of action. In the first year of the peace he made his name with *The Planets*.

Edward Wilson so far recovered from consumption after his visit to Davos that he became the most resilient of the party on two of Scott's Antarctic expeditions. He stood on the South Pole on 18 January 1912 and made one of his delicate sketches – of the black flag tied to an upended ski that told his party Amundsen had forestalled them. He died on the return to base, only a mile or two from safety.

Switzerland did not work the same miracle for James Elroy Flecker, another consumptive. A linguist, he spent the months before the war as a consul in the Middle East, but had to retire to Davos in 1914, where, after eighteen months ineffective treatment, he died. The news reached Cheltenham while Dr Flecker was preaching in Christ Church. After lying in state in the chapel of Dean Close School, the poet was buried in the cemetery under the Cotswolds.

In the depression that followed the war the new guide-books returned, with more evident desperation, to their image of an English Carlsbad, with long sections devoted to the four waters dispensed at the octagonal Pump Room in the Town Hall – the Fieldholme, or twinsalt; the sodium sulphate Lansdown, 'the water *par excellence* for anaemic dyspepsia'; the diuretic Chadnor; and that of Pittville, the only natural alkaline water in the country, which could also be drunk in the gardens of Pitt's Pump Room. But water could now be obtained in bottles anywhere and it was hardly necessary to go to Cheltenham to drink it.

The Medicinal Baths were highly advertised, bathing being now more popular than taking water internally. The pictures were daunting, in particular the room in which chronic alcoholics suffered treatment looked like a medieval torture-chamber. Vichy and Plombières Douches, Aerated Whirlpools, Irmessan, Foam and Brine Baths, Colonic Irrigation, Sedative Pools for the sleepless were all to be enjoyed or endured in the Bath Road. Besides boosting these amenities, the Town Council began its campaign to attract new industry to the area.

There had not been much of this at the turn of the century, apart from Boulton's and beer. The Cheltenham Press had been printing since 1836; Tilley's were making crumpets and brandy-snaps; the Victorian-founded firm of Larola turning out its bland white toilet milk; Beetham's manufacturing corn-plasters and glycerine-and-cucumber lotion; U.C.A.L., a group of chemists, making goods for sale to small firms.

One industry had been going on in the fields along the Tewkesbury Road from time immemorial, independent of factory buildings. The burler's teazel – *Dipsacus Sativus* – not to be confused with the native teazel, *D. Sylvestris*, was cultivated only in Gloucestershire and Somerset. 'Enormous quantities . . . were necessary to the clothing industry, the heads with their recurved prickles being used in the finishing process to draw out loose fibres from the cloth and raise a nap on the surface.' Attempts have been made to replace the field-grown product by wire combs, but in this instance nature still proves superior to man's invention. Buyers from Huddersfield came in September to offer for the 'chancy' crop, profitable only in dry seasons. The incredibly tough flower-heads, dried and threaded on combs or revolving 'gigs', were also used in the textile mills of Stroud. The Derrick family did not abandon their cultivation until the 1960s, when they were defeated by cheaper crops from France. A few are still grown in Somerset. A display in the Cheltenham Museum shows the stages of this historic industry.

Little building had been done in the town since the small-housed Victorian terraces that sprung up in the St Paul's and gasworks area. The Regency mansions were no longer suited to modern living and in spite of the slump there began to be a need for new housing on a modest scale. The first attempt to ease the shortage was by subdividing some of the big houses into flats, but in 1919 the Borough bought 116 acres in the parish of St Mark, a thinly populated 'select residential area', to build the first of the Council estates. The Mayor cut the first sod and the contractors moved in to dig drains, lay roads and build 600 new houses in generous gardens near the Gloucester Road. The new avenues, laid in a double horseshoe, were named after poets – Spenser, Milton, Tennyson, Shelley, Byron, Wordsworth, Kipling – the whole complex bisected by Shakespeare Road.

Earlier, in 1915 – a moment when war might have excluded all else from its mind – the Council had the imagination to buy five houses in the centre of 'that very superior range of buildings in the Sherborne Promenade' (Griffith, 1826) which are now the Municipal Offices. Since then they have bought eight more in the same terrace.

Hardly noticed by the inhabitants of the centre or the

fashionable 'villages' of Charlton Kings and Prestbury, Cheltenham was now getting its much needed new industry. Arising from Martyn's work in the Great War the Gloster Aircraft Company was formed and the long history of Gloster planes began, from the Gloster Grebes to the Gauntlets and Gladiators of just before the next war. Martyn's aircraft section moved from Sunningend to Brockwith in 1926, where the new company operated independently, later to become part of the Hawker-Siddeley Group. From the war years onward other firms began to arrive. One of these was the Aircraft Division of Smiths Industries (of Electrical Clock fame) and, in 1931, the Dowty Group. Sir George Dowty had been on the design staff of Gloster Aircraft, and he set up his own unobtrusive little workshop in a mews in the middle of Lansdown. In 1935 he moved three miles out to Arle Court on the Gloucester Road, a Victorian house which, though it replaced the demolished home of the Grevilles, had rescued and installed the original Elizabethan staircase and panelling. By the next war Dowty was employing 3000 people in factories in his grounds, making retractable undercarriages. The firm boosted Cheltenham's employment and set a standard for neat unobtrusive factory premises, away from the centre – a standard not upheld by all the industries that followed. Most of these also settled on the plain towards Tewkesbury and Gloucester and, while not achieving the elegance of Arle Court, managed nevertheless to build in such a way that the 1893 statement 'not a manufacturing chimney is seen' is still no idle boast.

The arrival of these industries enabled the Council to continue the work they had started with St Mark's Estate. In 1934 slum clearance behind St Paul's swept away some of the worst blots on the reputation of the Garden Town and 290 new houses were built there. Seventy more were constructed in Pate's Avenue, Alstone; a hundred at Pilley, off Leckhampton Road; 160 made up the Moors Estate, past St Peter's towards Tewkesbury; 720 houses were built on the site of Whaddon's Farm on the north-east. In 1938 the town's population was about 50,000.

All this building and slum clearance on the perimeter was little noticed by visitors or by parents arriving to take their children out at half-term to guzzle cakes at the Cadena Café in the Prom. They had probably travelled on the Cheltenham 'Flyer' – 75 minutes as far as Swindon, the fastest journey in Britain – arriving within a few minutes' walk of the town centre. If they went for Cotswolds excursions they climbed the hills on roads as yet unspoilt by suburban development. Nor was the growing factory-area likely to have been much visited by a young Cheltenham College master who first lived a hundred yards down the hill from the school and later at Charlton Kings. Unknown to anyone, perhaps least of all himself, the town was harbouring a second future Poet Laureate, though C. Day Lewis had not gone, like Tennyson, to improve his health with water. His aim was rather to improve the Classics and English of the boys of the Junior School, while finding time to raise a family and produce a volume or two of poetry. He quickly found that Cheltenham had not yet lost the conventional stuffiness of its reputation, and was soon in trouble for allowing himself to be seen painting his house in a green shirt and for appearing at a college concert in a stock. Worse was to come. His newly published volume, *Transitional Poems*, which, unlike Tennyson's works, *was* to be found in the local bookshops, was stigmatized with the awful word *sexual* by members of the staff and he had some difficulty in persuading them that the sentiments were innocent, since they were addressed to his wife. Cheltenham opened his eyes to the beauty of architecture and he was tempted to buy a Cotswold stone roofed cottage. The cost of keeping this in repair stimulated him to write the first of his 'Nicholas Blake' thrillers – *A Question of Proof* – and its success enabled him to shake the dust both of Cheltenham and of future classrooms off his feet. It also landed him in further trouble. The school of the story's setting was inevitably identified with Cheltenham Junior, himself with the hero, and the headmaster's wife, with whom the hero has an affair, with the wife of the new College Principal, Dick Roseveare. Fortunately Roseveare took the episode as an excellent joke.

At the time Day Lewis was at the College, Cheltenham was taking a good deal more interest in culture than when Tennyson was there, turning out his 'poetical effusions'. In the 1920s it boasted more societies, according to its guide book, 'than any other provincial town of its size – literary, artistic, social, historical, etc.' There were six cinemas, including one in the Winter Garden, and a screen in the Opera House, used for motion pictures when no live entertainment was available. There was music to be heard in the twenties and thirties, with a quintet playing every morning as the drinkers chose between the four different waters at the Town Hall – an attenuated echo of the morning 'band of musick' that annoyed Byng and diverted Wellington at the Old Well. The Thursday afternoon concerts listed newly famous names – Suggia, John Mac-Cormack, Clara Butt, Keith Falkner, Elizabeth Schumann, Myra Hess, Huberman, Marie Hall. Sabbath observance would no longer have impressed the Scots, even though the Town Hall's Grand Organ, given in 1926 to celebrate the Jubilee of Incorporation, joined with Cheltenham's orchestra of forty-two players for the Sunday evening concerts.

The year after was to see a celebration that did Cheltenham great honour. Gustav Holst's daughter wrote: 'The citizens of his native town . . . had an original idea. Instead of waiting until he died, and then putting up a stone monument to his memory, they decided to honour him while he was still living. They . . . hired the Birmingham orchestra, and gave a concert of his works at the Town Hall.' The first half of the programme consisted of four of his shorter pieces, some conducted by Adrian Boult. Holst himself conducted *The Planets*, a gruelling ordeal for one who was far from strong at the time. With Boult standing by, prepared to take over at a moment's notice, he got through the performance successfully. Cheltenham had sub-scribed enough money to provide nine hours' rehearsal for a two-hour concert – a gift particularly valued by a composer. The day was a tremendous success; the Town Hall packed. 'There were friends who had been at the Cheltenham Grammar School. There were choir-boys from Wyck Rissington, who were grandfathers by now. There were violinists who had played sonatas with Adolph. And little old ladies who had been passionately in love with Gustavus Matthias. There were even one or two, still older and more fragile, who had learnt their notes from Gustavus Valentine.' Holst called it 'the most overwhelming event of my life. It . . . has added many grey hairs – also inches! – to my head.'

Cheltenham's season was now a winter one, the new slogan being 'England's Favourite Winter Resort', as opposed to the summer one of Jane Austen's day. There were evening balls on Saturdays, enlivened by West End cabaret; almost daily Thés Dansants; Hunt and Race Balls continued. This came to a climax with the three-day annual race meeting in March, the major event of the National Hunt Season. The final event, the Cheltenham Gold Cup, first run in 1924, is the steeplechase equivalent of Royal Ascot and its true championship. The Grand National exceeds it in fame and in prize money, but is a handicap race, in which good horses have to concede huge weights to lesser runners. In the Gold Cup the contestants meet on level terms, the winner usually proving the best steeplechase horse of the year. The March meeting also includes 'Championship' races for novice horses, over hurdles and fences, long and short distances. The Champion Hurdle, run the day before the Gold Cup, is thought by enthusiasts to be the most competitive and exciting race in the calendar. Tradition is upheld by the inclusion of four races for amateur riders, one of which, the National Hunt Chase, over four miles, is known as the Amateurs' Grand National.

Racing history was made in 1932–6 when Golden Miller won the Gold Cup on five consecutive occasions, a feat that has never been equalled. The property of the Honourable Dorothy Paget, Golden Miller was the only horse ever to win both the Gold Cup and the Grand National. Prestbury Racecourse boasted its own little station and during Race Week ran special trains. 'It was nothing unusual', wrote one of their drivers, 'to have next to the engine a saloon with Miss Dorothy Paget and party. Miss Dorothy always had her own chef with her.'

To reach these winter attractions and the summer one of Cotswold country the guides and brochures did not omit to advertise the uniquely good communications. Apart from Prestbury Station, there were the three central ones, St James,

Road

Malvern and Lansdown Roads, and the suburban ones at
Charlton Kings and Leckhampton. Cheltenham could be
reached by three different routes from London – the present
Reading–Swindon–Gloucester way; by Oxford, Kingham and
Bourton-on-the-Water; or, the shortest way, by Honeybourne
and Winchcombe. The G.W.R. converged with the L.M.S.,
which went north through Birmingham; west by way of Bristol.
The Black & White Coaches, 600 a day in the 1930s, had their
station in St Margaret's Road, and drew in travellers from
as many places as the old stage coaches, and welcomed them
at their buffet with a cup of tea for 2*d*, according to the 1931
menu, a poached egg for 8*d*, or ham and eggs for 1*s* 6*d*. Few of
the hotels aspired to the grandeur of the Queen's, but there was
an ample supply, though they were not on a scale to attract
large tourist groups or business conferences.

When the Second World War put an end to ambitious projects everywhere, Cheltenham really seemed on the edge of
major reorganizations. It had been announced that the shabby
Winter Garden, opened with such *éclat* by Colonel Berkeley in
1876, was about to be reconstructed at a cost of £10,000 as 'a
modern pavilion, equipped with large Café, Art Gallery, Spa
Centre, Medical and Turkish Baths, Repertory Theatre,
Exhibition Hall and Sports Centre'. The Montpellier Spa,
apart from the banking hall, was in equally bad repair; Pittville,
used only for occasional balls and badminton, not much better.
What would have happened to these once glorious places had
Hitler never existed is no more than an interesting conjecture.

Numbers at Cheltenham College had risen now to 722. The
plan to build a war-memorial cloister had been shelved in
favour of a single covered walk, with names and a poem en-
graved in gold upon its walls, connecting the school to the
chapel. The rest of the subscribed money went to provide
scholarships for sons of old Cheltonians who had lost their
lives. The school acquired new playing-fields, the right of
access to a wooded park with views to the Cotswolds, new
College baths and a boathouse.

Pate's Girls' Grammar School was moved to new buildings
in Albert Road, Pittville, in 1939. At the Ladies' College Miss

Faithfull had been succeeded by Miss Sparks, during whose tenure of office the airy gymnasium was built and Miss Beale's centenary celebrated in 1931 by the opening of yet more boarding-houses. In 1934 the Principal received a little house of her own, built of Cotswold stone and facing north across the school quadrangle. The next head, Miss Popham, was honest enough to admit, 'I can't say that I ever grew to love it myself, for I felt that it was built too low and did not get much sun.' In 1935, before Miss Popham took over, the school was presented with the Royal Charter by King George V, the first to be granted since Queen Anne's reign, with a coat of arms in which the Guild's symbolical daisy was featured.

Margaret E. Popham, late of Westonbirt School, was a very different person from Miss Beale. Her first action after her appointment was to get herself booked for speeding in her car, a most un-Beale-like action. She was equally precipitate in school, running about the grounds, a thing forbidden to the girls. She walked the marble corridors unescorted, a thing never done by previous headmistresses. Her first innovation was to change the sober navy uniforms for the pale green still worn; the black stockings for brown. 'What is behind those walls?' visitors would ask, regarding the prison-like exterior on Montpellier Street, to be answered now by the statement – 'Quantities of young green ladies'.

It was while she was on holiday in the summer of 1938 that Miss Popham received a letter heavily marked 'Official Secret'. This informed her that all Ladies' College buildings were to be taken over in the event of war. She promptly invaded the Office of Works with the cry, 'You won't be defending Britain if you break up the public schools!' In January 1939 A. G. Pite, Headmaster of Cheltenham College, received a similar secret order. He was permitted to discuss it only with his President, Viscount Lee of Fareham, through whose assistance the entire school was found a home. The plan was kept dark till the last moment, when parents suddenly found themselves dispatching their boys to Shropshire, where Shrewsbury School put classrooms, labs, gym and playing-fields at Cheltenham's disposal. Dormitories they could not provide, so the boys were dispersed as lodgers all over the town, with consequent landlady problems, humorous and otherwise.

Being female and not predisposed to bow unquestioningly to authority, Miss Popham determined not to share the boys' exile. She went about the business of keeping her girls in Cheltenham craftily. Some went to local manors; Cowley, Brockhampton, Sevenhampton. Only seventy were banished to far Shropshire at Lillieshall Manor. She had the inspiration to fill the empty swimming-bath with water, rightly deducing that it would not occur to the Office of Works to requisition this. She did not tell them it could be floored over at a moment's notice. She phoned Bristol for twenty army huts, big enough to provide forty classrooms, and to the challenge, 'On what authority?' replied, 'We've just been taken over by the War Office and need twenty huts by 3 p.m. tomorrow.' She got them. Her school opened on the proper day with every girl provided with a bed, a desk and books. After six weeks Miss Popham was able to exchange the floored-over pool and the army huts for her own school building. Miss Beale could hardly have done better and would have done it with less subtlety.

The town returned to the frantic activity of the earlier war, but of a different kind. It was not refugees and wounded this time, but masses of healthy, lusty Americans. General John Lee, Eisenhower's deputy, practically took over Cheltenham for the Forces of Supply, himself at the Thirlestaine Hotel, his staff overflowing the 'temporary' government buildings at Oakley and Benhall, now the property of G.C.H.Q. Pittville Pump Room stored emergency rations in the ballroom, while the upper floors housed British and American soldiers. 'Generating stations were erected in the loggia, enormous Nissen huts fouled the greensward, and dry rot spread unchecked.'

Further Nissen huts, of the big 'Elephant' type, sprang up all over what is now Imperial Gardens, for, abandoning the grandiose plans of the thirties for reconditioning the Winter Gardens, the Council accepted a tender for their complete demolition in September 1940. The place once occupied by the palace of glass was quickly converted to a cooking-depot for the American forces.

Apart from the Americans, many British workers were evacuated to relative safety behind the Cotswolds and many light industries connected with essential war work joined the already existing aircraft manufacture of Gloucestershire, afterwards to remain for peaceful purposes. Most of the hotels were requisitioned; all the large garages taken over for aircraft works. Whittle's first jet engine was made at the Regent Garage.

The invasion of G.I.s caused the inevitable repercussions. The effect on the Cheltenham-born girl can be guessed from the history of many another English town, but the redoubtable Miss Popham was determined to protect her 'young green ladies' from anything undesirable. The American Red Cross was at the Queen's Hotel and large parties of its staff would collect between the Queen's and the College every lunchtime to watch the little groups making their way to their separate boarding-houses. 'I did the simplest and most direct thing,' Miss Popham wrote. She went into the Queen's, bearded the Officer in Charge and asked if she might address his men. He was dubious about this, but agreed to gather them in the lounge, where the headmistress, with almost underhand flattery, got the G.I.s on her side. Knowing, she told them, the Americans' great fondness for children, she virtually put the 'green uniforms' under their protection. Her girls were not allowed to talk, let alone to strangers, and she implored the co-operation of the soldiers. She won, as usual, and the lusty Americans became a silent courteous bodyguard to the little Ladies.

She reaped another advantage from her good relations with the troops. The enforced blackout made the Princess Hall virtually useless after dark, but the Americans wanted the hire of its stage for entertainments. Miss Popham let them have it free on condition they made it efficiently light-proof. She was rewarded with an efficient job and beautiful new curtains, and both school and army were able to use the hall throughout the war.

Miss Popham was proved right in her stand, for public opinion reinforced by the Headmasters' Conference, persuaded the Government it had been guilty of a blunder in taking over schools. The authorities decided to build a 'hutted camp' and return Cheltenham College to the premises from which it had been rudely ejected. There had been some amusement in the enforced exile. Shrewsbury boys had watched Cheltenham's play rugger; Cheltenham had shouted for Shrewsbury in their soccer matches. There was tobogganing in the winter term from the Kingsland heights and skating and ice hockey on the Common. But most people, staff in particular, were grateful to be back in May 1940, for the position of refugee is romantic only for a short time. They returned with a new young headmaster, faced with a financial deficit, the necessity of strict economy and numbers reduced to 470.

Having returned the children to their schools and later added to them with an influx of others from areas nearer the danger zone, as well as with expectant mothers and mothers of young families, the Ministry now turned its attention to inanimate objects and perpetrated a crime for which it will not be forgiven.

Cheltenham was a town full of metal – Regency wrought iron of unique design and delicate workmanship. Fortunately for posterity most of the balconies and porches were spared. But the Ministry made a vigorous assault on everything not actually attached to the fabric of the houses. Miles of roads were stripped of garden railings and gates; the ones surrounding Montpellier Gardens were uprooted and those along the length of the Promenade in front of the Municipal Office block. The high rails round the Winter Gardens also vanished. Last, and most unnecessary, the two Sevastopol cannons which stood outside the Queen's Hotel to commemorate Cheltenham's large contribution to the Crimean War were taken for scrap, leaving only the melancholy pedestals which still remain. This act of rape gave rise to the legend that the beautiful bits of metal were dumped in a field somewhere in the country to rot unused. It is certainly true that a huge pile of railings could be seen from the train between London and Cheltenham, arousing suspicion and fury. The truth or falsehood of this story will probably never be known.

CHAPTER THIRTEEN

Festivals Proceeding

THIS, as one used to say in the days when films were our weekly entertainment, is where I came in.

Arrived at the 1940s the town's biography must change its style. It is no longer possible to tell the chronological story among the bewildering forest of present-day facts. The forest presents itself as a convenient simile. In early and middle ages the road of history runs through open country, the events spread out, sometimes as thinly as one to a century, like single trees in the landscape. Around Elizabethan and Civil War times they begin to group themselves in roadside coppices and spinneys; in Regency days they arrange themselves at dimishing intervals along the way, until, after Victoria's accession, they form an orderly close avenue. Approaching the present day the biographer is brought up short on the edge of a thickly planted, partially impenetrable wood, choked with under-growth – the wood one cannot see for the trees. Any attempt at continuity must be abandoned to some biographer of the twenty-first century and the impersonal tone of history cast aside. The third person must be exchanged for the first so that the author can take responsibility for opinions on present building and future planning and the blame for the omissions that a book of this size must make.

Between the day when I bicycled wearily away from wartime Cheltenham, having been foiled of a train to Malvern, and the beginning of my post-war visits, what had been happening?

The Americans, to begin with, departed, starting their with-drawal from the moment of D Day. They left the sort of devas-tation that remains after occupation even by a friendly army –

buildings desecrated with pin-ups and graffiti; ploughed-up lawns; broken hearts; most serious for the town, the dry rot in Pittville Pump Room. On the whole they had not been un-popular, and the Ladies of the College may have missed their silent guardians. No place that has not developed a certain fondness for its invaders would unveil a tablet in the Town Hall recording their stay.

The prosperity that was to be the war's legacy in the new industries, with their promise of employment, was not immedi-ately noticeable to the casual visitor, to whom Cheltenham appeared as down-at-heel and shabby as most towns that had not actually suffered heavy bombing. Only the magnificent trees everywhere remained indifferent to the cataclysm that had shaken the world, as did the rooks that made their homes in them. But something quite new had, in fact, been in the planning for some time. Cheltenham had not been a leader of fashion since 1788 when the nation's papers had announced 'all fashions are completely Cheltenhamized . . . the Cheltenham cap – the Cheltenham bonnet' etc. But while most people had been exclusively busy with wartime matters, George Wilkinson, at the Town Hall, had his mind also on the future. Only five weeks after the war ended (May 1945) Cheltenham's first Music Festival was held, setting a fashion that was to sweep the country and continues to do so to this day. Not everyone remembers that Cheltenham's Festival began four years before Edinburgh's, six before Aldeburgh's. By the 1951 Festival of Britain there were eighteen. Now every city, town, borough and village feels uncomfortable if it does not have one.

G. A. M. Wilkinson was a Yorkshireman who became Entertainments and Publicity Manager at the Town Hall in 1932. During similar engagements at Harrogate and Buxton he continued the daily practice at his real ambition – to be a concert violinist – but by the time he reached Cheltenham he had decided his career was in administration. As the war went on he pondered schemes to make the town attractive to future visitors and in 1944 presented a report to the Entertainments Committee. This included the plan for a July Music Festival to last four days and to feature first performances by contemporary

British composers as its principal attraction. It was to be carried out war or no war. Largely through Wilkinson's enthusiasm the idea was approved and actually put into effect in less than a year. There were three concerts by the L.P.O. under Basil Cameron; Walton and Bliss came to conduct works of their own. There had not been time, in the first year, to find a new work, but Britten's *Sea Interludes* from *Peter Grimes* were given their first concert performance. Year by year the number of firsts increased, reaching their peak in 1960 with eighteen new works, by which time the festival had spread to two weeks. Its greatest period of glory was between 1947 and 1962 when Barbirolli regularly brought the Hallé Orchestra. The evening concerts were supplemented by afternoon chamber ones, by critics' forums and lectures, and, in 1949, the Festival was given its first formal opening service in St Matthew's Church, where, in successive years, various college choirs came to sing. For the first two years the Corporation was responsible for finance, but assistance inevitably had to be sought. When the Arts Council came to the rescue a non-profit-making company had to be floated, since the Council may not make grants direct to local authorities.

The story of the Festival is too long to tell here. Frank Howes published a history of the triumphs and troubles of its first twenty years. It is odd to discover the most *avant-garde* of all the festivals taking place in Cheltenham, but Wilkinson, a musician by vocation, was determined it should have a definite theme and chose a moment, the war having thrown us on our own resources, when a boost had been given to native orchestras, performers and conductors. English music had grown in popularity, with Vaughan Williams still prolific; Bax, Bliss and Walton established; Britten and Tippett near the start of their careers. Wilkinson retired in the spring of 1970. After some persuasion I extracted from him a letter on his own part in the Festival's creation. This ended, 'On more than one occasion the Festival has been described as "The Shop Window of British Music". I think it can be claimed with modesty, that the Cheltenham Festival for the last twenty-five years has done a good job for British Music and for Cheltenham.'

Like all artistic enterprise in this country, the Festival has its ups and downs. The B.B.C. broadcasts its concerts and frequently repeats them in Music Programme recordings in succeeding years. Many novelties are promoted to the Proms, though, inevitably, some first performances are also last ones. The peak of popularity for contemporary English composers has passed, the young ones of the moment turning out a kind of music not easily understood by any but the technically trained. The concerts include a few established classics, which bring in the Cheltenham resident who takes a pride in his festival but could not stomach a whole programme of the new stuff. Visitors come for the novelties and the fortnight's attractions include the sight of world-famous musicians wandering in the town. Recent additions are of outdoor jazz recitals and jollifications spreading to the sedate Promenade. Now there is a new glory in the reconditioned Pittville Pump Room, adding a concert hall that is beautiful not only acoustically but visually.

What do the residents feel about this modern festival in proverbially conservative Cheltenham? That I found difficult to discover. Some people affect never to have heard of it; others go into diatribes on the horror of the 'noises' they have not been to hear; many are pleased to see the visitors it brings but do not go to it themselves; but they do not go to the lengths of some Edinburgh people who spend eleven months boasting of their International Festival, then let their houses at a huge rent for its duration and go off to take their holiday. The schools patronize it, making one hopeful for the future. The majority of Cheltenham people, musical or not, seem proud that their Festival should be a matter of international, rather than of purely local importance.

Another, older, festival *is* principally of local interest. The Cheltenham Spa Open Music Competitive Festival (to give it its ponderous official name) has been going on since 1931, when, for a fortnight in May, individuals and groups from the surrounding counties – schools, villages and towns – sing, recite and dance for prizes awarded by well-known local names – the Dean Close Challenge Cup for Recorder Bands (under twelve years); the U.C.A.L. Cup for adult vocal quartets, and countless awards for verse-speaking, Greek dancing, solo instruments and madrigal societies.

It was largely the enthusiasm of the late John Moore that launched the Cheltenham Festival of Literature in 1949. Moore, as admirers of *Portrait of Elmbury* and *Brensham Village* know, was a Tewkesbury man. The Festival lasts a week in autumn and occupies the Everyman Theatre with a series of lectures, discussions and Brains Trusts, varied with excursions into something more theatrical in the shape of poetry recitals, illustrated talks on folk song and, in 1968, a full-scale drama – Micheál Mac Liammóir's *The Importance of Being Oscar*. The first year's programme opened with an address by Sir Arthur Bryant; talks by Nigel Balchin, Compton Mackenzie, Emma Smith, Ivor Brown and Peter Fleming; a poetry recital by C. Day Lewis (who can now read his own poems at Cheltenham College without anybody complaining of their *sexual* content); the week ending frivolously with a dialogue by Joyce Grenfell and Stephen Potter – *Hurrah for Books!* Literature is now incorporated with music in the non-profit-making Cheltenham Arts Festival Company. Until his retirement G. A. M. Wilkinson was prominent in its organization; Day Lewis is an honorary adviser. Like the Music Festival it has its ups and downs. John Moore kept its level upper-middle-brow to suit an audience that comes mostly from the Cheltenham, Gloucester, Cotswolds area. A literary festival cannot hope to attract the visitors who support the cosmopolitan art of music. Since Moore's death attempts have been made to raise its sights, for some of the early programme titles – 'My Favourite Book when I was Young' by Guest Writers – had an air of rather desperate scraping of the barrel and some Brains Trust personalities seem to have been dragged in for publicity rather than literary reasons. Some items are sparsely attended. A Victorian theatre is not the best setting for all types of discussion; not every author can speak as well as he writes or is trained to make his voice carry; some open debates have been heightened by a degree of insobriety that would make Dean Close turn in his grave. But when really good speakers as well as writers take the stage it is a different story. The first recital by Day Lewis after he was created Poet Laureate was crammed to the roof – 'everybody wants to see what such a creature looks like' was his own modest comment.

The Everyman, scene of the Literary Festival, is none other than Frank Matcham's little Opera House in Regent Street. As in many other towns television cut attendance at the theatre even more drastically than the films had done. The shortage of good touring companies after the war made it difficult to find anything to tempt the public away from the celebrities they could see on their private screens. In 1955 it was forced to close its doors. To the delight of the few who still cared, the Corporation decided to buy it, Cheltenham Council considering that, as the only 'live' theatre left in Gloucestershire, it was a public duty to keep it going. But not even they could make ends meet, and, in 1959, the peak of the TV boom, it had to close again.

A few enthusiastic locals; the film and music critics of the *Echo* – Derek Malcolm and Phil Jones; the recent director, John Gordon Ash; Margaret Davies of the Ellenborough Hotel (the scene of many Music Festival gatherings) and two or three others, met in a pub across the road from the deserted Opera House to discuss their dream of a nationally and locally subsidized rep. This discussion led to the calling of public meetings; the formation of a Theatre Association; the floating of another non-profit-making company and, on 2 May 1960, to the opening of an altered theatre with the new name Everyman (for Opera House was no longer applicable and had always been unduly grandiose) with a performance of a play by N. C. Hunter with Esmond Knight and Joyce Heron in the leads. The £12,000 raised had been used to enlarge the foyer, redecorate the charming interior and add new dress-circle and coffee bars. The big windows of the latter effectually destroyed the Victorian façade, but it had never been a thing of beauty and was more likely to put off than attract the youth of the 1970s. The Everyman is now supported by grants from the Arts Council, the Corporation and the County Council, the Urban or Rural District Councils of Charlton Kings, Cirencester, Stroud, Gloucester, Dursley, Newent and Tetbury, and by the Theatre Club of Painswick. In times of difficulty, which still arise, the

700 members of the Association rally to its help and have presented carpets, seats and black velvet tabs for the stage. A Young Everyman Group, dedicated to spreading interest in theatre through the County, has half-price tickets at weekends, organized visits to other Midland theatres, its own Drama Group and discussions in the Coffee Bar on Fridays. The YEGS make an imaginative contribution by organizing a baby-sitting service for house-bound would-be theatregoers.

A company numbering up to forty present a mixed repertory in which Agatha Christies and *Chase Me Comrade* pay for the thin houses of *The Long Day's Journey into Night*. The plays produced since it became the Everyman range from Shakespeare, Marlowe and other large-cast plays like *A Man for All Seasons*, through musicals like *The Boy Friend* and *The Young Visitors*, to Pinters and Weskers, all underpinned by revivals of the inevitable *George and Margaret* and *French without Tears*. Recently the YEGS distributed questionnaires to the audience and made the following discoveries – that 61·1 per cent were over twenty-five, with 31·2 per cent of the rest over and 25·7 per cent under twenty; that 51·4 per cent came from Cheltenham, with Gloucester and Stroud providing the next largest numbers; that 21 per cent of them attended every production. Somewhat disturbingly, in the management's view, they discovered that 90 per cent of their sample were satisfied with the choice of play.

A flourishing amateur movement leases the Everyman for two weeks a year for operetta and musicals, but it has its own permanent home, given by the Council in 1945. This is the playhouse in the Bath Road, a road called, by the way, after the city it leads to, not after the Municipal Baths which it housed. It was these Baths, so enthusiastically promoted in the 1930s, but now unable to compete with the National Health Service, that were converted into the theatre.

Having lost its Victorian Winter Gardens, to replace them with the more attractive lawns and flower-beds in Imperial Square, Cheltenham was soon to regain the use of its most impressive Regency pleasure-palace. When the Americans left Pittville and the Pump Room was de-requisitioned the dry rot was found to have penetrated far more deeply than first examination had suggested. The fungus had grown right into the brickwork behind the plaster, and the curved rafters supporting the magnificent dome were absolutely rotten. For a time it seemed the building was a total loss. Helped, however, by subscriptions from the public and from bodies interested in preserving fine buildings, a slow, thorough and apparently miraculous job of rescue has been done at a cost of some £53,000. The Pump Room was formally reopened by the 7th Duke of Wellington in 1960. His presence was appropriate, for the 1st Duke made daily visits to watch the building and to talk to some veterans of Waterloo who were employed on the work. The interior is newly floored, with its rosetted dome and arches painted in appropriate Regency colours. The huge hall is turned into a marvellous place for Festival concerts and gala occasions; the sunny upper rooms suitably leased to students of the Architectural Section of the Gloucestershire College of Art, whose own very modern building lies a little higher up the hill between Pittville and Prestbury. Hygeia, Hippocrates and Aesculapius, copied from the originals by Boulton's sculptors, once more crown the Ionic-pillared colonnade of what is surely the most beautiful Pump Room in the country. Inside the drinking-fountain was put in a new position, its well waters now pumped by electricity, and central heating was installed.

The older Montpellier Pump Room was also in a doubtful state. The Long Room, first rented, and then bought in 1926, by Lloyd's Bank, had at least been kept in use and preservation. But the Rotunda, with its separate entrance, was another matter. The waters had been gone for more than a century; its uses had descended in elegance – from balls to billiards to bingo. To prevent it being allowed to fall into further decay the Council purchased it in 1940, but, having recently spent a fortune on Pittville, was delighted when Lloyd's offered to buy the whole building to restore at their own expense if they might turn Thompson's great round ballroom into their central banking hall. Cheltenham hardly needed another such building, so the deal was completed in 1962. Lloyd's spent £100,000 on the work of rescue, Llewellyn, Smith & Walters of Knightsbridge combining with a firm of Gloucester builders on the delicate problem of restoring the copper dome from the outside so as to make no disturbance to the plaster-work of the interior. The hall now contains a circle of counters under its beautiful ceiling, from which depends another circle of severely tubular lamps – a combination of the modern with the Regency that I cannot feel is successful. The outside is once more neat and handsome, even with the modern lettering 'Lloyd's Bank Limited' running along the colonnade under Thompson's pleasantly self-satisfied white lion, which gazes proudly across at Montpellier Gardens. The caryatids, north and south of the bank, are well preserved and make a uniquely pleasant walk, enclosing between their ample silhouettes a collection mostly of antique shops and boutiques, though the effect is marred here and there by an unnecessarily ugly snack bar or launderette.

For a town of Cheltenham's long history there are remarkably few statues. There is, of course, the bronze of Wilson in the Promenade and the unusual plaster likeness of William IV, rather unsuitably presented to the town where his callously discarded mistress, Dorothy Jordan (mother of his ten children) had acted so successfully. But just upwards on the hill past what must be the most beautiful branch that Lloyd's Bank possesses, stands, in the middle of the road, a very unusual monument. This shows Edward VII, informally dressed in knickerbockers and Norfolk jacket, gingerly holding the fingertips of a pretty little barefoot waif, who shyly regards the King's stout sensible shoes, while his other hand rests on her shoulder.

CHAPTER FOURTEEN

A Time to Build

It took Cheltenham a little time to discover the change that industry had brought it. In the middle of the town was a good deal of dilapidation. On the outskirts a certain amount of jerry-building had inevitably taken place to provide quick accommodation for families temporarily housed during war-time, who then discovered they were here to stay. The Cheltenham Society, formed to save the Regency heritage of the town, agreed, to the surprise of many, that some of the less distinguished older buildings should be pulled down in order to concentrate their resources on restoring the best. One side of Pittville Street was totally removed to make way for shops, as well as old buildings in Winchcombe Street. The beautiful spacious terraces of Lansdown and Bayshill are one by one being cleaned and put in order. One plan, which would have doubled the beauty of the town centre, had to be abandoned to the demands of big business. It was suggested, in 1955, that buildings should be demolished to open up a view of the parish church and that this should be looked on as a war memorial. The scheme would have made a vista from the Promenade to Cheltenham's oldest building and its pleasant graveyard, which is completely hidden from view. Enthusiastically supported by people of all denominations or none, the plan was defeated because it would have entailed the removal of two commercial buildings in Clarence Street, but a demolition there in 1970 (made simply in order to build new and better offices) gave a glimpse of how successful this project would have been. But in Cheltenham, as in other places, big business sometimes triumphs over civic pride, as was shown when Eagle Star put up its skyscraper between the College and Montpellier Gardens – a modern building by no means ugly in itself, but out of scale with its surroundings and ruining the proportions of Imperial Square and the distant view from above Pittville.

Another tragedy is the loss of Dr Jenner's house in St George's Place. With the exception of Edward Wilson, with his statue in the Promenade, an inscription beautifully cut in the Cotswold stone of his parents' house in Montpellier Terrace, and a some-what grim block of flats named after him in the suburbs, Cheltenham's famous have not been extravagantly honoured with plaques and street names. Holst had that splendid concert in his lifetime, but his name was not put on his home for fifteen years after his death; the plaque to Fred Archer is fixed to the wrong house. There are, of course, the inevitable tributes to the Berkeleys and Duttons of Sherborne on roads built in the days when compliments to noble benefactors were necessary to a town's prosperity. Captain Skillicorne, the Spa's founder, is remembered in a little walled garden, enclosing his bust, behind the Town Hall. Flecker's name does not appear on the street plan; 'The Close' in Hester's Way does not, pre-sumably, commemorate the Dean, but he has, of course, his school. Miss Beale recently acquired both a Road and a Walk, but the former is only four houses long and the latter, little more than a pathway, inappropriately skirts the playing-field of a boys' school, more than a mile from her beloved Ladies' College. It is, however, a great deal longer than the little suburban passage that commemorates one of Cheltenham's greatest benefactors – de Ferrières Walk.

The story of Jenner's second house is typical of the conflicts between progress and preservation that arise in a town which is both historical and expanding. The first he lived in, Alpha House, some way out across the railway, is now the head-quarters of Spirax-Sarco, makers of steam traps and heat-transfer equipment, who have put a record of his occupation on its well-preserved exterior. When I started to collect material for this book his more famous residence, 8 St George's Place, which must have been a charming Georgian house, stood mouldering away. Now it has gone, and the stranger could not even guess where it once stood, for Cheltenham's Regency Harley Street has been renumbered. Councillor Paul Saunders fought desperately to save it for posterity, but it was a losing battle and engendered much bitterness. There were accusations that the advocates of progress took tiles off the roof and broke windows while the controversy raged, so that rain and pigeons could get in and settle the matter in their favour. Probably most towns could produce parallel stories, whether true or false, in the universal conflict between the claims of the new against the old.

The war had caused a six-year gap in the Council's housing programme, which began in 1919 with the purchase of the ground for St Mark's Estate. Soon after the peace building activity was resumed on a vastly expanded scale. The need for this acceleration was the growth of industries that had arrived before and during the war and a stream of new ones seeking sites and accommodation for their workers. Dowty's, developing on various new lines, had overflowed Arle Court and had new factories elsewhere in Gloucestershire with the Dowty–Rotol merger making propellers at Staverton, the little airport between Gloucester and Cheltenham. Smith's Industries were developing Bishop's Cleeve into a small town; Walker, Crossweller (arrived in 1937) had a huge, well-designed factory at Whaddon, for thermostatic mixing-valves and shower-bath equipment; Telehoist make hydraulic tipping truck-bodies; there are brewers, nylon-spinners, paper, plastic and chemistry manufacturers. When, at the beginning of the 1960s, Walls, the largest ice-cream makers in the country, wanted to settle in Cheltenham, no room could be found for them and they had to go to Gloucester.

Homes were also needed for the personnel of that skyscraper – the Computer Division of Eagle Star; for the corresponding division of the Royal Insurance; for the Universities Admission Council, moving from London to offices in Rodney Road. But the greatest spur to building came from the arrival of a mass of Civil Servants. Government Communications Headquarters, a department of the Foreign Office engaged in research, development and production of communications equipment, was transferred from London in 1952. This new invasion was housed, for its working hours, in those 'temporary' buildings at Benhall and Oakley which had been the wartime base of the American Forces of Supply – two sites on opposite sides of the town. These newcomers, with their wives and families, needed adequate living accommodation. The Council undertook to provide 500 new homes and an equal number of single flats to attract a type of new resident who, they hoped, would make a contribution to the town's activities, social, civic and artistic.

The Council housing programme, interrupted by the war, was resumed with the construction of the Lynworth Estate, next door to Whaddon. Then the builders returned to the St Mark's area, site of the first Borough Council housing experiment. Next to its streets named after eight English poets, Rowanfield was built – a rectangle of avenues named after ten English counties. The largest, latest and most ambitious of the estates, almost a new town in itself, is Hester's Way, between the Tewkesbury and Gloucester Roads, and crossed by the wide sweep of Princess Elizabeth Way, with its shopping-centre in Coronation Square – names which mark the date of its construction. Here are 3000 new dwellings, from large blocks of flats to semi-detached two-storey houses, as well as the schools, churches and chapels necessary for the vastly expanded population, including Cheltenham's second Roman Catholic church, the hexagonal building dedicated to St Thomas More. With 550 temporary buildings being replaced by permanent houses on the other side of the town and new developments south in the Hatherley district, the Council owns, in 1970, 7235 houses and flats, 5527 of which have been built since the war. Private enterprise is responsible for a roughly equal number.

Cheltenham's present population is about 80,000, not sufficient to qualify it for County Borough status. If Charlton Kings and Prestbury, both outside the Borough boundary, were to attach themselves, the numbers would reach the qualifying figure of 100,000. But the inhabitants of the thatched-roofed, half-timbered houses and cottages of these areas cling to their identity as separate villages. The principal directions in which the town has spread in the last hundred years are westwards, where almost all the houses beyond the railway have been added; north-eastwards, between Prestbury and Hewlett Road, and south of the Park and Hatherley Brook. A great deal of building activity has recently begun on the north, where Swindon Lane is rapidly losing its country character, its orchards, fields and pigsties and its open view to the Cotswolds, and becoming another suburb. I watch the spoiling of this pleasant drive round the town's northern perimeter with regret, as many before me must have mourned the loss of farms and orchards that existed where Hester's Way now stretches its miles of 'little boxes'.

Facts and figures make dry reading. It is more interesting to visit the new estates and find out what they are like to live in. In course of time even the vast one at Hester's Way may come to look as if it stood there by right, for, though the trees now planted are no longer the great planes, chestnuts and evergreen oaks of the Regency planners, the Council has kept faith with its reputation as the Garden Town, though they have, perhaps, an excessive enthusiasm for pink cherries. Alongside the new pavements vast acres of grass verge have been planted, an admirable idea so long as there is time and labour to keep it mowed. At present the grass is all too often ragged-edged and full of dandelions blowing their clocks into neighbouring gardens. Princess Elizabeth Way is a magnificent broad road, but grim as yet with the red brick blocks of Scott and Wilson Houses not yet softened by age. Coronation Square, full of supermarkets and Do-it-Yourself shops, has the impermanent air of a frontier town in a new country; buildings that look like piles of matchboxes contrasting strangely with the oriental–Russian dome of the Grammar School across the way. Nearby, as always in Cheltenham, is a green space – the pleasant Hester's Way Park, with roses, azaleas and heathers, enhanced by the science-fiction radar instruments of Benhall rising beyond its trees. On a fine day after school it seems as if every house in the streets around has half a dozen children, all the smaller ones on tricycles in the middle of the roads, while the larger ones busy themselves vandalizing the phone boxes, none of which are in working order for more than a day at a time. Alarm at this undue population explosion is mitigated by a walk through the older estate of St Mark's, where hardly a child is to be seen, the people who found homes on this first Council enterprise being now past the age for rearing families. Here, also, the trees are well developed, the gardens mature, giving one hope for the future of the newer suburbs. Literally a stone's throw from the endless semi-detacheds of Hester's Way one can turn down Fiddler's Green Lane and find oneself among fields and haystacks.

In search of something more sophisticated than the shops that new estates provide, the young families cram the Saturday buses or push their pramloads of children (half-suffocated and totally invisible under parcels on the way home) towards the Promenade, whose shops, in response to the demands of Cheltenham's new population, now close early on Wednesday and stay open on Saturday afternoons.

When the London institutions, both industry and Civil Service, were confronted with the prospect of moving beyond the Cotswolds, the first question asked by many of the wives was – 'What is the shopping like? Will I find my familiar stores?' – in particular – 'Will I find a Sainsburys?' The High Street had long ago possessed its Woolworths and Marks & Spencers, but it was only in the last few years that two Tescos appeared, and in 1968 the requested Sainsburys was ceremoniously opened in the presence of Lord Sainsbury himself. It, and one of the Tescos, stand side by side on the ground once occupied by Pate's Grammar School. The site had belonged to the Fellows of Corpus Christi, under Pate's Foundation of 1586, and they maintain an agent in Cheltenham to look after the rest of their property. This includes the pleasant Victorian houses of Henrietta Street and a row of well-designed little brick villas, built by the foundation in the 1930s, in St Paul's Street. The income from Pate's properties goes to endow a lectureship in divinity at the college in Oxford. The Fellows sold the site of the Grammar School, on a valuable corner of the High Street and it was pulled down in 1967. The excellent supermarkets that replace it can hardly be said to add to

Cheltenham's visual beauty, but the Street has lacked charm ever since the days when the primrose-edged stream ran down its middle. The Victorian Tudor building that replaced Pate's first school was hardly an ornament.

But the ancient Grammar School was not to be lost. In April 1965 it had already moved to the suburbs – to that sombre brown building with the dome alongside Coronation Square. It took with it the original parchment in which Richard Pate had entrusted the foundation to his college, but, inexplicably, dropped his name, becoming Cheltenham Grammar School and severing one of the most ancient links with the town's pre-Regency history. Bryan Little, the architectural writer, thinks the new school one of the town's best modern buildings, but it seems odd these days that anyone could design a school so dark inside that even on a sunny day most of the classrooms have their lights perpetually burning. The school numbers 840 pupils. There are 750 at the girls' equivalent, above Pittville, which, oddly, since even the enlightened Pate did not dream of educating females, does preserve his name in *its* title – Pate's Grammar School for Girls. Nobody knows the future of these schools in the present Comprehensive battle, for discussions are still going on between the Governors and the Local Education Authority.

There is no space to do more than bring the histories of the more famous schools up to date, though many have been built in the new suburbs to keep up with the influx of population. Numbers have risen at Dean Close, with added boarding-houses along the Lansdown Road. Numbers and prosperity returned to Cheltenham College after its brief wartime exile. In 1947 the school made itself a magnificent addition by buying next-door Thirlestaine House, with the wings that once housed Lord Northwick's pictures. This great mansion provides accommodation for bachelor masters, a waiting-house for boys not yet allotted places in the school's eight boarding-houses, living- and changing-rooms for day-boys, six classrooms, art rooms, a language lab., a prefects' room and, in the Long Gallery, a place for art exhibitions and music. The extra space enabled the original Big Modern to be redesigned as a library by Louis de Soissons, a perfect room for quiet study. Three science labs were built round the central Quad. Big Classical had to be re-roofed in 1950, and the opportunity was taken to rake the floor and install a permanent stage, a switchboard copied from Stratford-upon-Avon and a film projector. The emphasis on preparation for the Army is lessened – the former Classical and Military Divisions remaining only as the names of opposing rugger teams. Instead of the pre-war preponderance of Classics and languages, with a minimum of maths and science, now about half the school studies science and medicine, a third history, and a mere handful Classics. Hobbies, lacking before the war, are numerous – pottery, carpentry, hi-fi, drama, the orchestra. The College acquired over seven acres of useful land behind its new addition. 'This means there is a walk to the Junior under the huge old cedars of Thirlestaine House, and through the walled kitchen garden, as well as a large and tolerably safe lawn for small children to play on.'

At the Ladies' College Miss Popham had been succeeded in 1953 by Miss Joan Tredgold, who remained for eleven years. The appointment of the present Principal, Miss Margaret E. Hampshire, was a surprise to many, not least to herself. Tall, dark and good-looking, she was in no way connected with education before a friend half-seriously drew her attention to the fact that Cheltenham Ladies' College was advertising the post. She was looking for a change from the responsible position she held at Courtauld's and decided to apply 'for fun'. She was accepted; her appointment being among the first of a series of similar ones by large schools, who began to turn to the organizing ability of industry for their headmasters and mistresses. The school now possesses twelve houses, mostly scattered about Bayshill and round the handsome tower of Christ Church. Each is in the charge of a housemistress and it is here school life apart from games and lessons is passed. The girls attend Sunday service in the church of the parish where they live, providing an infusion of youth to the congregation and some lively singing. A degree of supervision still in force would not have displeased Miss Beale; for example, girls may not travel on public transport or go to the theatre or cinema without permission; nor may they write letters to anyone not on a list supplied by their parents. On the other hand they mix with the opposite sex of Dean Close School (what would he have thought?) for the performance of plays and choral works.

St Paul's Teacher Training College, started in 1847 in Daukes's Victorian Tudor Quadrangles, had originally been co-educational (a very early essay in mixing the sexes) as far as classes went. Now only the men remain, the women having left their nearby house of residence to go half across Cheltenham to their own establishment, St Mary's College in the Park, in 1921. Additional buildings for them were opened there in 1962 by the Queen Mother. The outskirts of the Park is also the home of the North Gloucestershire Technical College, whose inmates, along with those from the College of Art above Pittville, have combined on occasions of student protest to bring Cheltenham into the popular movements of today.

The vast and growing youth of the town will soon be able to pass its leisure hours at a new Sports Centre, imaginatively designed by Mr G. A. Jellicoe, in process of construction on the open space that rises towards the Race Course between the western edge of Pittville Park and Tommy Taylor's Lane. The traditional sports continue, with Rugby Football at the Athletic Ground, very central in Albion Street, and Soccer a little further out at Whaddon; from the wrought-iron balconies of Suffolk Square one can watch the members of the Cheltenham Bowling Club (one of several) whose little pavilion is in the middle of the gardens. The Cheltenham Cricket Club has its headquarters at the Victoria Ground in the Battledown district, and there are many smaller clubs. To turn to more illustrious matters, the Cricket Festival continues, and, since the days of the Three Graces, Gloucestershire County Cricket Club has sent many famous names to play on the College field – Dipper, Hammond, Goddard, Parker, Graveney, Mortimore and Procter among them. In 1969 Gloucestershire came second in the County Championship. The 1960s were notable at the Prestbury Race Course, when the incomparable Arkle, who is said never to have fallen or to have run a bad race, won the Gold Cup in three successive years (1964–6) and would probably have doubled that figure if it had not been for the injury that ended his career.

It was in 1964 that rumours were confirmed that Cheltenham's stations were to be reduced to one. Various lines, particularly the charming slow ones, were already suffering the fate of small railways all over the country, and on those that remained the smaller halts were being shut down. Two years of protest were to follow, but it was clear from the start that individual opinion had little hope of stemming the extraordinary official passion of the 1960s for taking as much traffic as it could off safe and easily regulated railways to put it on inadequate and overcrowded roads. Certain private individuals, like those who burnt the life-sized effigy of the Minister of Transport outside Cirencester station on 5 April, evidently thought it worth a gesture. The line to Kingham, one of the three to London, had been closed for two years. The Cotswold Line was no more, only one or two stations being kept for freight. Charlton Kings and Leckhampton had been shut down, the residents of the latter 'village' protesting at the plan to turn over to industry the site of their abandoned station. By December 1964 it was revealed that Malvern Road and the terminus, St James, would be the ones to go. Cheltenham, said officialdom, was not a junction and did not justify more than one station. Though plans for closures had, in theory, to be approved by the Transport Users Consultative Committee, there did not look to be much hope for the objectors. Lansdown was, for geographical reasons, the most obviously convenient for British Rail, being on the main route from the North to Bristol, South Wales and the West, with trains to London as well. But it was far from the town centre, and far from elegant to look at since the loss of Daukes's pillared portico, which had served to shelter passengers from the rain as they waited for their carriages in the nineteenth century. Now plans were drawn up for extension of the platforms, and improvements in the waiting- and buffet-room facilities. The usual 'alternative bus service' to the town centre was to be provided. Objections came thick and fast in letters to the *Echo*; the bus service was 'a bad joke', there being little space for luggage on buses, which were anyway notorious for never running to time. Lansdown is one of the most dilapidated stations I have ever seen,' said another correspondent in 1964 – a statement that was still true early in 1970.

Services were to be withdrawn from the other two in January 1966, by which time, it was promised, Lansdown would have undergone 'general improvement'. The Assistant Town Clerk, Richard Board, insisted, 'Cheltenham must have a station which is worthy of the town as a holiday and health resort', and pointed out that, as things were, there were no washing facilities, the waiting-room was Victorian and the platform too small for the thirty or more extra trains that would come each day, bringing about 2000 extra passengers. Anybody who travels to Cheltenham today may wonder what became of British Rail's promise. At last, in March 1970, scaffolding was put up and a start made on scraping down the flaking paint on the despoiled façade and putting on a new coat. But behind its shining new portals, the waiting-rooms remain Victorian and are all on one side of the line. There is a pleasant welcome, however, good tea and coffee and excellent home-made cake in the tiny buffet, though one asks in vain for beer or spirits.

The Council announced an ambitious plan to convert the station area at a cost of about £250,000, with a new hotel (Cheltenham had lost about thirty since before the war), a dozen shops, restaurant, filling-station and a parking-space for 200 cars, but this had to be abandoned, owing to a 'temporary cut back in expenditure'. With the St James's site to be bought, and the coming problem of the new Town Plan, Cheltenham Council must have had already more than enough on its mind.

The Honeybourne line managed to stay open longer than most of the small ones. Its closure put an end to the Race Specials to Prestbury Station which, accordingly, went out of service at the end of the Race Week of March 1968.

CHAPTER FIFTEEN

The Town Plan

IN the middle of the 1960s the Ministry of Transport required all towns with a population of over 50,000 to prepare a plan to cope with traffic problems for the next decade. Not having the status of a County Borough, Cheltenham's Plan had to be drawn up by the Gloucestershire County Council, and was not, therefore, the work of people who knew the town from the inside.

The first alarming suggestion, that a trunk road should be driven across the centre, south of the High Street, bisecting the Promenade, Regent Street and Rodney Road, was quickly disposed of, but the final Plan, produced in May 1966, was not much more pleasing to some members of the Council, the mass of private citizens, or, particularly, to the Cheltenham Society, whose principal *raison d'être* is the preservation of the Regency town.

The defects of the Plan are now a matter of history, and dryish history at that, but they must be recorded for the sake of completeness and to show the kind of disaster that could happen as a result of too hasty decision. Reference to the present town map will help to make its proposals clear.

Its main 'improvement' was the creation of a four-lane distributor-road, linked to inner roads, swinging round and enclosing three-quarters of the town, with a pedestrian precinct in the centre. The new road was to approach from the south-west by way of the Gloucester and Lansdown Roads, turning to skirt Montpellier Gardens, to be joined, on the corner of the Bath Road beside Cheltenham College, by another main road from Leckhampton. The new road then swept north between the Bath and College Roads through the middle of Sandford

Park, where it was planned to cover it with a multi-storey car-park near the site of Barrett's Mill. Crossing the High Street, it went north again, skirting the Athletic Ground and curving west below Pittville Circus to another multi-storey park over York Street, before crashing its way through a complex of streets between St Margaret's and St Paul's Roads, stopping short of St Paul's Training College. Then it plunged south to the St James's Station site in a curve that crossed the High Street and returned to it at the junction of the Gloucester and Tewkesbury Roads. The portion of the High Street inside the ring, from St Paul's Street to the corner of Sandford Park, with the Promenade as far as the bottom of the Municipal Office block, and the parts of Winchcombe, Pittville and North Streets below Albion Street, were to be reserved for pedestrians. St James's Station would be developed for industry and another large space in the town centre, the back yard of the Plough Hotel, would become a new shopping-area. The plan was submitted to the Ministry of Transport in July and in the spring of 1967 a public inquiry was held.

There were no lack of objections: from people who saw their pleasant homes about to be swept away in the interests of traffic or feared the proximity of the new, noisy, petrol-smelling road would ruin their peace. The High Street and Promenade of this once salubrious town were already made unpleasant by fumes from lorries unable to avoid it. Their removal to a faster road, running in so tight a circle round the centre and involving the destruction of beautiful houses and the trees for which the town is famous, did not seem a happy solution, besides failing to provide the much needed bypass from Oxford to Tewkesbury and Gloucester. There were complaints from sources easily foreseen; from the College, faced with the prospect of a noisy, dangerous road junction cutting off the corner of its attractive grounds; from the Everyman Theatre, carefully preserved in the central area, but with no means of access for lorries delivering materials for scenery. The strongest protest came, inevitably, from the Cheltenham Society, which viewed the destruction of the town's architectural treasures with dismay, and foresaw the total ruin of its character as a spa.

In the municipal elections of 1967 the representation on the Council was altered to the extent that the objectors carried the day and the Plan was thrown out, as far as Cheltenham was concerned. Two years later, taking local opinion into account, the Minister of Transport finally rejected the County Council's Plan and recommended that consultants should be appointed to start work on another. Sir Hugh Wilson and Mr Lewis Womersley are now making an investigation expected to end in 1971 and to cost £53,000, of which Cheltenham and Gloucestershire will pay a quarter each and the Government the rest. The firm of Wilson & Womersley, besides planning new towns, is doing similar work on other places of historical interest, including Brighton and Exeter, their object being to preserve the character of the town centres while improving the flow of traffic around them. It is they who are leading the inquiry into alternatives to the passionately disputed suggestion of a road through Christ Church Meadows in Oxford. Sir Hugh Wilson, President of the R.I.B.A. for 1967–9, told the Cheltenham press he was 'very excited about the whole project' and said it was the greatest challenge he had faced in many years of dealing with problems of the kind.

But nearly six years will have been wasted, with an incalculable sum of money, not only for the cost of the rejected plan, but also the loss of valuable rates from the fifteen acres of St James's, now reverting to a grassy meadow. A state of 'planning blight' has existed, nobody wanting to buy or being able to sell because of the uncertainty of the future, and there are shops, especially in the threatened roads north of the High Street, waiting empty and unlet.

Welcoming the planners in May 1970, the Mayor, Alderman Miss May Dent, deplored this loss and delay. She appealed to everyone to adopt a reasonable attitude, if they wished Cheltenham to survive as the principal commercial and shopping-centre of the North Cotswolds. 'It is no good saying what is not wanted. What we require now is for people to come forward and say what is wanted. We have to cope with the motor car and at the same time retain the Regency charm of Cheltenham.'

The visitor from larger, more commercial, cities may be forgiven for wondering if the apparent panic about traffic is not a little exaggerated. Even before the Cheltenham Borough Council's own traffic-management plan – for an anti-clockwise one-way system round the centre – has been accepted by the Ministry of Transport, it appears to flow more easily than it did in the period immediately after the war, and those who worry about it should try to drive into Bath at the weekend, where one can spend an hour covering a mile and a half, or on the roads round Exeter in summer.

One reason why traffic conditions seem better than in many towns is that the Council has always recognized that parking-space is of great importance in a regional shopping-centre. Cheltenham was the first town in Britain to adopt the continental disc parking-system – a system so successful that it is to be extended. Eight surface car-parks have been provided, all near shopping-centres, at a cost of £300,000. The town was again a pioneer in the 'Trust the Motorist' car-park scheme, at sixpence a day. In this case the motorist proved unworthy of the Council's confidence, and car parks are now controlled by automatic barriers at a daily fee of a shilling.

Mr D. G. Williams produced a critique of the rejected Plan for the Cheltenham Society and a list of alternative recommendations that ought to satisfy most people who are not simply concerned with profit. While it recognized that something should be done to lessen the danger to health, physical and mental, that traffic brings, it proposed putting the road much further out and suggested use could be made of the obsolete railway lines, a measure that would cut down costs and avoid the destruction of people's houses. It deplored the multi-storey car-parks so near the town centre, detracting from Cheltenham's character. It begged the Council to think again before importing new industries into the St James's site. Like the clergy, the Society would prefer to attract more people to live there, to avoid creating a ' "tombstone" centre of office blocks, dead in the evening', like the City of London. With the new road at a decent distance, a reasonable one-way traffic-system, and the pedestrian precinct suggested for the Promenade and High Street, Mr Williams, like Mr Bullock, hopes for new developments along the lines of Cheltenham's past. 'Backed by the Cotswolds, and originally planned for rest and recreation, if properly developed the town could become a great centre for conferences and seminars and pull in a far higher percentage of the world's expanding tourist trade than it does at present.'

The Society's recommendations included plans for keeping as many cars as possible out of the centre, residents only being allowed to park in their own sectors. People coming in to work would be encouraged to leave theirs in garages on the perimeter and make use of a new system of single-decker buses. Bicycles, I am glad to note, *might* be permitted 'into certain of the central area roads and allowed to cross sectors'. Mr Williams expressed a pious hope, which must be echoed by all who use it, that Lansdown Station would be fully modernized by British Rail. His suggestions for St James's are ambitious. Underneath the site his report proposes a vast bus-terminal, to which all the long-distance systems could be moved. This would set free a large area in North Place, home of the Black & White Coaches, for housing or shops, and remove one of the most lamentable blots on the town centre – the dreary semi-circle of bus shelters that surround the magnificent plane trees in front of Royal Crescent. Cheltenham's oldest Georgian houses, that once looked on to Skillicorne's Well Walk, could then be restored to something like their original charm. On top of St James's underground bus-station the Society suggests the building of a conference centre; an hotel and exhibition buildings, a few shops and offices, together with some places of recreation, such as an ice rink or swimming-pool – the last perhaps less necessary, with the new Sports Centre being built on the corner of Pittville Park. 'Around the perimeter of the site,' the report goes on, 'especially overlooking the River Chelt side . . . would be a high density, low rise family housing area. . . . The whole character of the St James's site could be developed as a new Tivoli – gay and fun-loving.'

For the Cheltenham Society, a young woman, Felicity Roberts, made a survey of the River Chelt and produced a document describing 'this insignificant stream' from its entrance through Charlton Kings in the east to the garden recently developed by the Parks Corporation west of the town along the stretch that flows parallel to the Tewkesbury Road – the attractive Chelt Walk. This and the part that runs through Sandford Park, '12 feet wide and flanked on either side by willows', are the only places where the river is generally seen by the public. In fact, as Miss Roberts makes clear, with the exception of a few places where it plunges under streets, the longest being below the Promenade and the A.B.C. Cinema (the site of the removed Imperial Spa), it is possible to follow the stream right across the town. Though partly hidden and in need of cleaning, much of it is already pleasant; a breeding-ground for mallard, its banks covered with wild flowers. The stretch beside the College Baths is redolent of wild garlic on a hot midsummer day. There is a tree-lined, dark, mysterious stretch between the backs of the houses in St George's Place and the St James's waste land. Further on it becomes invisible behind walls, the running water only to be heard, and there are notably unpleasant parts, both to eye and nose, in the gasworks area. Miss Roberts hoped that more of this rivulet could be developed as it has been in the Chelt Walk near Hester's Way. Recently the Cheltenham Society enlisted the help of Youth Action on this project, and young people have spent their weekends clearing the stretch by the College Baths to replant the banks with appropriate trees, shrubs and flowers, as a contribution to Conservation Year.

After looking at the parish church, the Pittville Pump Room and the Montpellier Rotunda with its attendant caryatids, the Regency terraces and Promenade shops, the visitor to Cheltenham could find pleasant diversion in pursuing this river with a map. The journey would reveal a cross-section of the town in all its periods and states of development, from the splendid to the squalid, and, by the end, he would have seen something that few who have spent their lives there have ever thought of exploring. Another place that he must visit, perhaps before setting out on any expeditions, is the new Cheltenham Room in the Museum and Art Gallery. Here Mr G. H. Fletcher, the curator, arranged, in the summer of 1970, a comprehensive permanent exhibition of prints and photographs of Cheltenham in all periods of its history.

From places to people – the most striking thing to many visitors is the almost total absence of coloured faces in the streets. The very rare black one will belong to a tourist, or to someone over for a day's shopping from the West Indian colony whose back gardens can be seen from the London train in the suburbs on the far side of Gloucester. The few brown faces belong to a community of a dozen or less Indians and Pakistanis from the Tewkesbury Road direction. To a visitor from cosmopolitan London or the industrial Midlands this lack almost gives Cheltenham the effect of being a foreign town.

On the other hand variety is supplied by the dress and hair style of the hippies, to be seen on seats along the Promenade or in the parks, eyed with suspicious care by the police. Though Cheltenham has its 'heads' who take the occasional trip on L.S.D., they are mostly pot smokers, the hard drug addicts, I am told, being of an older generation and living in colonies on the Cotswolds. Most of Cheltenham's two hundred from behind the restored façades of the Regency terraces go out to work of some kind, the 'dole' not being prepared to support them indefinitely. The Corporation Parks Department employs a number; some work for Walls Ice Cream at Gloucester, at the local aluminium factory, or help to make new motorways. Hardly any find non-manual work, for there are few shops or offices in Cheltenham that would not insist on conservative dress and 'short back and sides', but their activities seem peaceful and the ones I have spoken to articulate and responsible.

Another touch of colour is provided by the town's one or two notable eccentrics. Your safety may be endangered by a lady who arrives at great speed on her bicycle, in the middle of the road or on the pavement, shouting and waving her arms in the air and suddenly leaping off to let her machine continue its progress without her. Or you may have the fortune to meet, in the town centre, a woman who pushes a load of miniature white dogs in a perambulator, and wears a ground-length dress of white lurex festooned with fur stoles and covered, in winter, by a long white velvet cloak, the overflow of dogs trailing behind on leashes. At weekends you may be unfortunate enough to witness a battle between the police and invading Hell's Angels or skinheads, though this, one hopes, may be a passing fashion. More pleasantly, on Sunday evenings on the way to Evensong, you may meet, and be tempted to follow, a really excellent Salvation Army band.

With the exception of the parish church and St Matthew's, the Catholic churches and Christ Church, which I have always found open, church visiting is not too easy. The variety of places of worship of all denominations and styles of architecture is as rich as it was in Regency days and worth the trouble of exploring, but most are locked on weekdays, the effect of the same sort of vandalism among Cheltenham youth as makes it hard to find a working phone-box in the new estates. A visit to a service or an approach to a churchwarden may be the only means of getting inside.

Church attendance seems high by present standards, St Mary's being full and cheerful at mattins, especially when the sun is strong enough to penetrate those sombre windows. An equally large congregation seems lost in the vastness of St Matthew's, where parish Evensong is held. The magnificent 'Gothic' Christ Church has allowed some of its splendid Victorian memorials to be obliterated behind its new organ, but it has an attractive modern extension, with rooms for social and parish meetings, brightly decorated, and including something rarely provided by any church – cloakrooms for Ladies and Gents. If the suburban churches are not quite so well attended as the central ones they provide a friendly welcome to the stranger, with introductions and offers of lifts home. The hexagonal Catholic St Thomas More's has a glass-enclosed section where mothers can take their babies to see and hear without themselves being heard – a practical idea also incorporated in the design of the Baptist church at Hester's Way.

The parish church, the oldest piece of Cheltenham, hidden away among its narrow alleys, is an essential pilgrimage for visitors. Outside it stands the ancient preaching-cross, several times broken and restored, under which John Wesley is thought to have delivered one of his sermons. There are a variety of tombstones with inscriptions well known to the collector; one, for instance, to a blacksmith –

My sledge and hammer lies reclined,
My bellows pipe have lost its wind,
My fire's extinct, my forge decayed,
And in the dust my vice is layed,
My coal is spent, my iron's gone,
My nails are drove, my work is done.

and one to somebody who must surely have been a Georgian
descendant of Mrs Baghott-Higgs of Jacobean ill-fame –

Here lies John Higgs,
A famous man for killing pigs,
For killing pigs was his delight
Both morning, afternoon and night. . . .
His knife is laid, his work is done,
I hope to heaven his soul is gone.

There is something else not everyone in Cheltenham has
noticed. Let into the path that runs diagonally across the
churchyard are three narrow strips of blackened brass, the
ancient measuring device dating from the days when Cheltenham's thriving market was held near by. Here, in the shadow of
the church, purchases of rope and material could be checked,
in a place where no one would dare to cheat.

St Mary's modern history continues at the centre of Cheltenham's life and since Canon Hugh Evan Hopkins became
Rector its field of work has been extended as well as its premises.
The Rectory is in Wellington Square, Pittville, but in 1961 the
parish was able to buy No. 1 Crescent Terrace, a Georgian
house no distance from St Mary's on the corner of Royal
Crescent, with funds raised by a Stewardship campaign which
succeeded in doubling the church's income. A recent legacy
made it possible to pay off the mortgage on the building. Here
the Rector and his two curates have their offices and the
Cheltenham branch of the Samaritans is housed.

Suicides take place here as in other places. Cheltenham, with
its old and new towns and their different types of society, provides, among others, two groups particularly prone to depression – the elderly retired and the younger victims of 'New Town
blues'. The local Samaritans started in 1963 under the Rector,
exactly ten years after the Reverend Chad Varah started his

movement in the City of London and the year in which it received its Charter of Incorporation. Canon Hopkins does not insist on church membership or even on religious conviction in his team of Samaritans, believing that even the avowed atheist can be as capable of helping his neighbour as the professed Christian if he is sympathetic and practical. Details of such work are obviously not for publication, but at least a dozen people come to Church House every week for advice on some problem or other.

Radical changes are taking place in the town as I end this book. To the dismay of older residents, both members and outsiders, the New Club, which had stood for just under a hundred years on the corner of the Promenade and Imperial Square, and was noted in the past as the haunt of the ultra-conservative element, has come down to be replaced by a five-storey office-block with a basement park for nearly a hundred cars. The purchase price was £111,000 and the cost of redevelopment will be about £500,000. Made wary by the controversy over the Eagle Star 'skyscraper', the developers called in the Royal Fine Art Commission to ensure that the new design would not spoil the proportions of the Promenade. Meanwhile such of the club members as did not resign in dudgeon have been rehoused in comfortable new premises at the top of a Regency house north of Montpellier Gardens.

Mr John Bullock, the new Entertainments Manager, a Manchester man of thirty-five, has, like George Wilkinson, spent his career up till he came to Cheltenham, in similar employment – as Assistant Business Development Manager for Belle Vue in his native city, and as Publicity and Entertainments Manager at Shrewsbury and St Albans. Wilkinson will be remembered in national as well as local history for the creation of the Music Festival. Bullock's particular ambition, as I have indicated, is in publicizing the town for the tourist trade. The Victorian slogan, 'The Centre for the Cotswolds', will be re-emphasized; but Cheltenham itself, with the restored Pittville Pump Room, ought to be able to attract far more of the mass of visitors who daily, from March to November, hurtle in coachloads from London to Stratford-upon-Avon and Warwick

Castle. With the imminent junction of the M4 and M5 motorways not far from the town and better roads everywhere this should create no problem. Hotels and new restaurants are badly needed and will, it is to be hoped, be included in the plans for St James's Station.

When I started work upon this book there was, as I said in my Introduction, not one drop of water to be had from the Town Hall fountain. It was one of the first important events in John Bullock's Cheltenham career to see the restoration on 11 July 1970 of its claim to be called a spa.

Two years before, when that fatal storm sent diesel oil and the overflow of Pittville Pump Room sewage into the existing well, there were a good many people in the town – the ones more concerned with industrial and commercial progress – who rejoiced in the idea that the loss of the water would put an end to Cheltenham's outdated reputation for bath chairs, old ladies and gouty colonels. But the Borough Council was not anxious to sever its links with the past and allocated £3000 to drilling for water again. George Stow and Company Ltd, waterworks specialists from Henley-on-Thames, advised by a consultant geologist, started boring at a place a hundred yards from the polluted well. There were moments of anxiety when the drill had penetrated 120 feet of the clay without result and Alderman A. Dodwell, Chairman of the British Spas Federation (a fast dwindling body) had a sleepless night fearing he was going to be made to look 'a proper Charlie'. But in the morning came a phone call with the news that water of a kind unique in Europe had been found 138 feet below ground.

Though this water is not yet available to the public a 'tasting' was included in the ceremonies of the annual Regency Rout – a private party consisting of an Olde English dinner at the Plough, followed by a ball at the Pittville Pump Room, the guests in Regency dress. The water, 'chlorinated up to the hilt' had not yet been analysed or pronounced fit for human consumption and some reluctance was shown by the Borough Surveyor to provide the necessary bucketful. Cleaning of fissures in the well had necessitated the recent pouring in of 400 gallons of hydrochloric acid. A tray-load of glasses was,

however, released, and circulated to local dignitaries under the
chandeliers of Pittville's beautiful ceiling. The guests bravely
downed it, Mr John Jeens, a solicitor, dressed as the Regent,
declaring, 'I'm sure it will do me a tremendous amount of
good, as it did my dear father.' It is on record that he grimaced
– but water was probably never Prinny's favourite drink, and
there have been no reports of ill effects on any of the guests.

The new well, behind a piece of ground destined to be a car
park, has been fitted with a pump and will, when pronounced
safe, be supplied direct to the Old Spa Well at Pittville. The
Town Hall's water will have to be transported by road. It will
be available free to the public at both places.

So Cheltenham is going to be a spa again. How many extra
tourists will the news attract? It is certainly of historical interest,
and the local water, which I tasted shortly before the disaster, is,
unlike the warm 'Epsom salts' of Carlsbad, which Cheltenham
once sought to rival, perfectly palatable. But I wonder if a
public enthusiasm for water-drinking could ever be revived.
For many decades there have been two factions in the town –
the one clinging to the title Cheltenham Spa, preserved on the
railway tickets, the Welcome notices and the Town Hall
writing-paper; the other seeking to banish it with its outdated
Victorian image, and putting, as the Municipal Office station-
ery does, Cheltenham *tout court* as its letter heading. I do not
wish to take sides. My own explanation for this book's title is
that it starts at least a thousand years before the pigeons drew
attention to the spring in Mason's field, and even if Cheltenham's life has been fuller and better documented since Captain
Skillicorne built his pump-room that is by no means the whole
of the story.

Bibliography

The Diary and Letters of Madame D'Arblay, 7 vols (1842–6)
The Letters of Jane Austen, ed. R. W. Chapman, 2 vols (1932)
Dorothea Beale, *A History of Cheltenham Ladies' College* (1904)
Bernard Blackmantle, *The English Spy* (1826)
Edith Brill, *Old Cotswold* (1968)
John Byng, Viscount Torrington, *The Torrington Diaries* (1934)
The Life and Letters of Lord Byron, ed. Thomas Moore (1838)
Thomas Campbell, *A Life of Mrs Siddons* (1839)
Cheltenham, the Garden Town of England (Cheltenham, 1890 and 1893)
The Cheltenham Pittville Pump Room (Cheltenham, 1960)
Cheltenham Guide, 1781–1968
William Cobbett, *Rural Rides* (1830)
Hope Costley-White, *Mary Cole, Countess of Berkeley* (1961)
John Fosbroke, *A Picturesque and Topographical Account of Cheltenham, &c.* (Cheltenham, 1862)
The Gentleman's Magazine (1788)
John Goding, *Norman's History of Cheltenham* (Cheltenham, 1863)
S. Y. Griffith, *A Historical Description of Cheltenham* (1826)
Philip Guedalla, *The Duke* (1931)
Gwen Hart, *A History of Cheltenham* (Leicester, 1965)
Geraldine Hodgson, *J. E. Flecker* (1925)
Imogen Holst, *Gustav Holst* (1938)
Frank Howes, *The Cheltenham Festival* (Cheltenham, 1965)
Josephine Kamm, *How Different from Us* (1958)
Felicia Lamb and Helen Pickthorn, *Locked-up Daughters* (1968)
C. Day Lewis, *The Buried Day* (1960)
Bryan Little, *Cheltenham* (1952)
Elizabeth Longford, *Wellington: the Years of the Sword* (1969)
Simeon Moreau, *A Tour to Cheltenham Spa* (1783)
M. C. Morton, *Cheltenham College* (1968)
Pate's Grammar School (1852)
Margaret E. Popham, *Boring – Never!* (1968)
Paul Saunders, *Edward Jenner: The Cheltenham Years* (1969)

John Sawyer, *Cheltenham Parish Church* (Cheltenham, 1903)
George Seaver, *Edward Wilson of the Antarctic* (1933)
Lady Shelley, *The Diary of Frances, Lady Shelley* (1912–13)
J. W. Street, *I Drove the Cheltenham Flyer* (1951)
John Wesley, *The Journal of John Wesley* (1903)

The 2½ inch to the mile (1 : 25,000) Ordnance Survey map
covers Cheltenham on sheets SO 91, 92.

Index